INTEGRATION AND COMMUNITY BUILDING IN EASTERN EUROPE

INTEGRATION AND COMMUNITY BUILDING
IN EASTERN EUROPE

Jan F. Triska, series editor

The German Democratic Republic
Arthur M. Hanhardt, Jr.

The Polish People's Republic
James F. Morrison

The Development of Socialist Yugoslavia
M. George Zaninovich

The People's Republic of Albania
Nicholas C. Pano

THE GERMAN DEMOCRATIC REPUBLIC

THE
GERMAN
DEMOCRATIC
REPUBLIC

ARTHUR M. HANHARDT, JR.

THE JOHNS HOPKINS PRESS

Baltimore

FOREWORD

T*he German Democratic Republic* is part of a series of monographs dealing with integration and community building in the communist party states of eastern Europe. These monographs are further part of a larger program of studies of the communist system sponsored by Stanford University.

It seems appropriate here to outline the theoretical and methodological concepts that were developed for the series as a whole. The focus has been on the communist-ruled states as part of a loosely structured community or system—its origins, development, and internal behavior. The major underlying assumption is that each communist party state has characteristics peculiar to it that predispose it toward varying degrees of co-operation, co-ordination, and integration with the others. We think that the present behavioral characteristics of the system can be traced to environmental, attitudinal, and systemic factors, and that we can learn a great deal from a comparative analysis of the process and degree of integration of each member state into the community of communist party states—whether, for example, the process involves force or consent, similar or shared institutions and codes of behavior, or whether integration is effective at elite levels and/or at lower levels as well, and so on.

The concept of political integration and community formation and maintenance is, as a focus of intellectual curiosity and investigation, as old as the study of politics. The mushrooming of supranational integrational movements since World War II has given a considerable new impetus to the old curiosity and has changed the emphasis of the investigations. Social scientists, who in the last two decades have been building a general theory of political integration, whether on a subnational, national, or supranational level, have been perhaps less concerned with the philosophical content of the concept of integration than with discovering operational indicators that would endow the concept with empirical meaning and allow the theory to be tested for validity and reliability. The principal centers of their inquiry have been two broad independent variables, *interaction* and *attitude*. Although in most cases investigated separately, interaction and attitude are assumed to combine to constitute a community, the objective of the process of integration.

The principal subjects of inquiry have been transactions across the boundaries of states and attitude formation within them. The theorists stipulate that the number and density of transactions among states indicate the degree and nature of their relationships. Flow of mail and telephone traffic; trade; aid; exchange of tourists, officials, and migrants; cultural exchange of persons and communications; newspapers, periodicals, and book sales and translations; radio, TV, and motion picture exchange; mutual treaties and agreements; and common organizations and conferences are the kinds of indicators that, measured and plotted over time, should demonstrate the direction of integrational trends and developments.

With reference to attitude formation, theorists have been more concerned with the process of integration than with its results (conditions) within states. The pertinent literature yields relatively little on this subject. In *Nationalism and Social Communication,* Karl Deutsch argues that it may be fruitful to study two sets of persons within a unit of analysis: those "mobilized" for integrational communications and those "assimilated" into the new, larger unit. If those assimilated multiply at a more rapid rate than those mobilized, then "assimilation" is gaining and "community is growing faster than society."

At present enormous problems are involved in studying the results of the integration process in communist countries. It is difficult to assess attitudes because of the great sensitivity of officials and decision makers, and it is either difficult or impossible to obtain reliable aggregate and survey data. This informational problem makes it correspondingly difficult to develop a general theory of integration or to make systematic comparative analyses. We have therefore been compelled to rely on indicators of degrees and trends, a method that depends considerably on subjective judgment and inference.

Although the data available are uneven in quality and quantity, our approach has been rigorous and systematic. Each author was asked to examine the country under review with reference to five historical periods: (1) the precommunist stage before the country became a party state and hence a member of the system; (2) the period of the communists' consolidation of power after World War II when the states of eastern Europe entered the system; (3) the subsequent era of repression and rigid controls; (4) the period of relaxed controls following Stalin's death; (5) the last ten years. For each of these periods, as appropriate, the author was asked to identify and analyze the phenomena relevant to his country's integration in the system: its ecological-physical features, its demographic structure, belief system, social system, degree of autonomy, its dependence on other states, and its hopes, needs, and expectations with regard to integration and development. Within these broad confines, each author was asked to emphasize the periods and events with the greatest significance for the integrational development of the country in question. It is our feeling that a more rigid set of prescriptions would have been self-defeating in view of our objectives and the exploratory nature of our undertaking.

Although the major purpose of Professor Hanhardt's study is to examine the role of East Germany in the communist system, it can also serve as a useful introduction to any student of the country. Still, as in the other studies in this series, the major focus is on that behavior of the German Democratic Republic (G.D.R.) relevant to integration and community formation with its neighbors and friends in eastern Europe, in particular with the Soviet Union. "Is the G.D.R. such a slave to the Soviet Union that it is uninteresting, or is East Germany so unique among the allies of the Soviet Union that its experience cannot be generalized to the others?" asks Hanhardt. He answers that it is neither. The East German integration into the communist party state system has been selective, bilateral, and although "mainly" with the Soviet Union, it shows increasingly less dependence on the U.S.S.R.

One final remark of a general nature is in order. The series is based on the assumption that although the countries of eastern Europe are now gaining more freedom to conduct their own affairs, they do not reject the need for association among themselves as such. All the communist parties in power in eastern Europe find real and necessary the idea of a world communist community united in opposing capitalism and in carrying out its historical destiny. All of them, we believe, would find it instinctively repugnant to do anything that could precipitate a final, total break with the communist system.

This series is an intellectual product of many creative minds. In addition to the authors of the individual monographs—in this case, Professor Arthur M. Hanhardt, Jr., Department of Political Science, University of Oregon—I would like especially to thank Professor David D. Finley of The Colorado College and Stanford University for his original contribution and assistance.

JAN F. TRISKA

Institute of Political Studies
Stanford University

CONTENTS

Foreword   vii

Introduction   xv

Abbreviations   xxi

Map   xxiii

1: THE PRE-ENTRY PERIOD:
1945-49   3

2: THE ENTRY OF THE G.D.R. INTO
THE COMMUNIST PARTY STATE
SYSTEM   43

3: THE INTENSIVE SOCIALIST
DEVELOPMENT OF THE G.D.R.   55

4: THE THAW:
1956-60   67

5: THE PRESENT STAGE:
1961 AND AFTER   77

6: EVALUATION: TRENDS
AND PROSPECTS   107

Appendix: Selected Data Tables   115

Selected Bibliography   125

INTRODUCTION

The purpose of this brief monograph is to introduce aspects of the development of the German Democratic Republic (G.D.R.) in terms of its integration into the international communist state system. An introduction seems necessitated by the fact that relatively little has been written in the United States about East Germany. Indeed the German Democratic Republic receives scant attention in comparative politics texts and series. Whether or not this is in deference to American and West German policies of nonrecognition—until very recently the G.D.R. has been referred to as the Soviet Zone of Occupation—must, for now, remain a matter of conjecture. However, it is clear that the G.D.R. has been classified between the realms of Western and Eastern European studies, with each specialty claiming that the land between the Elbe and Oder-Neisse belongs in the province of the other.

More important than the possible effects of diplomatic policy or the fences separating fields of academic specialization, is the allegation that the G.D.R. is not worth studying. The major proponents of this point of view hold either that the G.D.R. is such a slave of the Soviet Union that it is uninteresting, or that East Germany is so unique among the allies of the Soviet Union that its experience cannot be generalized to the others. Whatever validity this view may have had disappeared with the growing economic importance of the G.D.R. after 1953 and with the closing of the Berlin sector border August 13, 1961.

The German Democratic Republic is the most important trading partner of the Soviet Union. Although this relationship has increased East German dependence upon the U.S.S.R., it has also strengthened the hand of the G.D.R. in dealing more independently with Moscow. This was recently illustrated in the negotiations leading to the 1965 trade treaty—no longer did the G.D.R. meekly acquiesce to Soviet demands. Even though the agreement signed in December can be held as being more advantageous to the interests of the Soviet Union than to the G.D.R., its terms were probably less exploitative than those proposed at the outset of negotiations. In the final analysis the superior East German per capita GNP is no match for Soviet size, total output, and, ultimately, Red Army divisions. Nonetheless the East Germans are aware of their hard-earned prominence and are acting with accordant self-assurance.

The construction of the Berlin Wall in 1961 gave the G.D.R. the same degree of control over its population as was held by the other members of the Soviet Bloc. As in the Berlin uprising of June 17, 1953, the Western powers and the West Germans did not intervene. This compounded the feelings of isolation and disillusionment among the East German people. After initiating strong measures designed to cope with possible unrest following August 13, the G.D.R. leadership relaxed controls in 1962, realizing that the popular mood was one of resignation rather than rebellion. In the years since 1962 resignation has been transformed into a sense of "state loyalty and pride" based on undeniable East German accomplishments in the face of immense difficulties. The material aspects of life in the G.D.R. have improved and as people look eastward comparisons appear increasingly favorable.

The eastward orientation of the G.D.R. is in part a function of its integration into the system of communist party states. Frequent references will be made to factors that have enhanced or inhibited East German incorporation and integration. The incorporation into the Soviet Bloc was an outcome of World War II and the breakdown of interallied co-operation after 1945. The Soviet Zone, as a result of policies and counter-policies, became the German Democratic Republic in October, 1949, shortly after the British, French, and American zones had been transformed into the Federal Republic of Germany. From 1949 on the East German communist leadership instigated changes that made the G.D.R. institutionally harmonious with its bloc partners.

Although there is some controversy about the "spill-over" effect of economic integration into the political sphere, it is clear that such carry-over has been encouraged by the East German communist Socialist Unity Party (SED). The SED has had a continuity of leadership under Walter Ulbricht that is unparalleled in the Soviet Bloc. Ulbricht's career, from its beginnings with the establishment of the Communist Party of Germany, has been one of absolute loyalty to Moscow. Ulbricht's loyalty, combined with his political capabilities, has helped the integration process from the German side.

East German integration into the communist party

state system has been selective, bilateral, and mainly with the Soviet Union. COMECON has been helpful in integrating the East European communist states, but the degree of integration has not been as wide as was hoped, partly because socialist economies were not as easily melded as had been anticipated. Resurgent national policies have done their share to disrupt integrative efforts. Further, the differing levels of development among the East European states led to a selective interrelationship among the most developed—the U.S.S.R., Czechoslovakia, and the G.D.R. These states stand out in the pattern of bilateral pacts that characterize bloc relations. The multilateral agreements that would be expected in conditions approaching international integration are few and far between.

The economic primacy of the Soviet Union in the external relations of the G.D.R. is in good measure a function of the division of Germany. Intra-German trade patterns before the war indicated a dependence of East Germany on the raw materials from Western Germany and from the eastern territories that are now part of Poland and Czechoslovakia. The prewar trade channels have not been adequately reopened since 1945, and the G.D.R. has been forced to produce such raw materials as it can and to become a leading customer of the Soviet Union.

Perhaps the comparative aspect is the most fascinating in the gradual integration of East Germany into the communist system. As the G.D.R. develops and matures as a socialist state it becomes further estranged from the Federal Republic—out of a common political culture two new polities are emerging as the Republics integrate into the Eastern and Western state systems. In the West the middle class, liberal democratic order is being carried forward. In the East the socialist and communist traditions of Marx, Engels, and the Communist Party of Germany within the Communist International are being developed in what might be called a long-term revolution. The changes in class structure and class opportunity in East Germany have been profound as have the alterations in the economy.

All this is not to gloss over the human cost and suffering resulting from a divided Germany. Many have been tragically affected by what is called the "German Problem." I have interviewed individuals shortly after they have made good an adventurous scaling of the Wall. The histories of individual and familial fates are deeply moving. However, there is no end to division in sight. And as long as there are two Germanys, they both deserve our attention.

I should like to thank Professor Peter Christian Ludz, Freie Universität, Berlin; Professor Arthur M. Hanhardt, The University of Rochester; Randal L. Cruikshanks, University of Oregon; the Archives of the Ministry of All-German Questions (Bonn); and the Office of Scientific and Scholarly Research of the University of Oregon Graduate School for their help and support. Of course the responsibility for errors of fact and interpretation remains mine.

Arthur M. Hanhardt, Jr.

Department of Political Science
University of Oregon

ABBREVIATIONS

CDU	Christlich-Demokratische Union *Christian Democratic Union*
COMECON	Council for Mutual Economic Aid
DBD	Demokratische Bauernpartei Deutschlands *German Democratic Peasant's Federation*
DFD	Demokratischer Frauenbund Deutschlands *Democratic Woman's Federation*
DIN	Deutsche Industrie-Normen *German industrial standards*
DK	Deutscher Kulturbund *German Cultural Federation*
FDGB	Freier Deutscher Gewerkschaftsbund *Free German Trade Union Federation*
FDJ	Freie Deutsche Jugend *Free German Youth*
KPD	Kommunistische Partei Deutschlands *German Communist Party*
LDPD	Liberal-Demokratische Partei Deutschlands *German Liberal Democratic Party*
LPG	Landwirtschaftliche Produktionsgenossenschaften *Agrarian Collectives*
NDPD	National-Demokratische Partei Deutschlands *National Democratic Party of Germany*
NVA	Nationale Volksarmee *National People's Army*
SED	Sozialistische Einheitspartei Deutschlands *Socialist Unity Party*
SMAD	Sowjetische Militäradministration in Deutschland *Soviet Military Administration in Germany*
SPD	Sozialdemokratische Partei Deutschlands *Social Democratic Party*
TGL	Technische Normen, Gütevorschriften und Lieferbedingungen *Abbreviation used for DDR-Standards* *or industrial norms*
VDGB	Vereinigung der gegenseitigen Bauernhilfe *Peasant's Mutual Aid Union*
VEB	Volkseigene Betriebe *People's Enterprises*
VVB	Vereinigungen Volkseigener Betriebe *Associations of People's Industries*
VVN	Vereinigung der Verfolgten des Naziregimes *Union of the Nazi-persecuted*

The German Democratic Republic

1: THE PRE-ENTRY PERIOD: 1945-49

On April 30, 1945, a Soviet military aircraft left Moscow and landed on an airstrip near Frankfurt-on-the-Oder. The passengers were members of the "Gruppe Ulbricht," German communists who had survived the Great Purges in the Soviet Union to become the executors of Soviet plans for postwar Germany.[1] The leader of the group, Walter Ulbricht, as the most important individual in the Communist Party of Germany (KPD) and later of the Socialist Unity Party (SED), was to supervise the Sovietization, and therewith the eventual integration of a considerable portion of the former German Reich into the communist party state system. Ulbricht remains to this day a remnant and a reminder of the Stalinist era that he personifies.[2]

The Communist Party of Germany and later the Socialist Unity Party that emerged from the forced unification of the KPD and the Social Democratic Party of Germany (SPD) co-operated closely with the

[1]Wolfgang Leonhard, *Die Revolution entlässt ihre Kinder* (Köln: Kiepenheuer und Witsch, 1955), chap. 7; and Leonhard, "Es muss demokratisch aussehen . . .," *Die Zeit* (North American Edition), no. 19 (May 14, 1965), p. 8.

[2]Carola Stern, *Ulbricht: A Political Biography* (New York: Frederick A. Praeger, 1965).

Soviet occupation forces to control the political situation in East Germany after the capitulation. Nonetheless, the period of the Antifascist Democratic Order that extended from the German surrender to the founding of the German Democratic Republic (G.D.R.) in October, 1949, can be termed the pre-entry period. The hope of extending communist control to other zones of occupation was kept alive for at least the first half of the period, finally dying with the formal establishment of the Federal Republic of Germany in September, 1949. This hope, while it lasted, necessitated a minimally co-operative posture on the part of the German communists in dealing with groups that transcended the borders of the Soviet Zone. That political groups other than communist had some autonomy at that time and that the communists exhibited a measure of co-operation with these groups are distinguishing features of the pre-entry period.

Ecological–Physical Factors [3]

East Germany contains all or parts of the former provinces of Brandenburg, Mecklenburg, Pomerania, Saxony, Saxony-Anhalt, and Thuringia. The total area of the G.D.R. is 108,273 sq. km., or 23 per cent of the 1937 Reich. East Germany is less than half the size of the Federal Republic, which covers 245,283 sq. km. (The East German-West German area relationship is roughly that of Tennessee to Oregon.)

[3]Since the ecological-physical features of the G.D.R. have remained quite stable, the current description will not be repeated in subsequent sections. Data will cover all time periods. Unless otherwise noted, sources for this section are Gerhard Schmidt-Renner, ed., *Wirtschaftsterritorium Deutsche Demokratische Republik,* 3rd ed. (East Berlin: Verlag Die Wirtschaft, 1961); and *Statistisches Jahrbuch der Deutschen Demokratischen Republik.*

On the north the G.D.R. borders on the Baltic Sea, the principal seaport being Rostock, which has been developed intensively since 1945. The G.D.R. is the westernmost of the European communist party states, reaching to 9° 54′ E. The long common border with the Federal Republic of Germany has fostered a "front line" mentality among East German communists that is something of a mirror image of West German feelings of being a bulwark against communism.

Although there have been many consequences of a divided Germany, one of the most important has been its disintegration as an economic unit. (Table 1 indicates the dependence of East German industry on the products of West Germany by showing the percentages produced in the East prior to World War II.) This has made the integration of the G.D.R. into another economic system a matter of survival. Given the international constellations of East and West following the war, the only economic area available to East Germany was and remains the Communist Bloc. East German economic integration, at first a matter of direct exploitation through Soviet reparations, gradually became one of bilateralism within the eventual framework of COMECON. Although multilateral integration has been a goal, the U.S.S.R. has in effect taken the place of West Germany and the eastern provinces of the Reich as a source of raw materials and trade. The neighbors of the G.D.R. to the east and southeast— Poland and Czechoslovakia—have become, after the Soviet Union, its most important trade partners. Yet the G.D.R. has been somewhat isolated from its eastern neighbors since no amount of socialist reconstruction or socialist brotherhood can eradicate the mutual memories of war and occupation.

The G.D.R. consists of generally hilly to mountainous terrain in the southern portions (Thuringian Forest, Erzgebirge) and the southwest (Harz). In the central region the land flattens into a lake and marsh area north of Berlin. Over this surface is stretched a tight communications network. The over-all density of the rail network is 150 km. per 1,000 sq. km., with a range of 78 km. (Neubrandenburg) to 1,194 km. (East Berlin). The major concentration of rail connections is to be found in the industrial districts south of Berlin. Complementing the rail network is a system of navigable rivers and canals. The major rivers—the Elbe, Spree, Oder, Neisse, Havel, and Saale—which are not naturally connected, have been linked by a system of 473.7 km. of canals to produce 2,000 km. of usable inland waterways. The density of the road network for the G.D.R. over-all is 408 km. per 1,000 sq. km. The range in the Bezirke of the G.D.R. is from 236 km. in Neubrandenburg to 753 in Karl-Marx-Stadt (formerly Chemnitz). These figures do not include the 1,378 km. of Autobahnen and do not include Berlin.

Demographic Structure

Population and its distribution. The structure and distribution of the East German population have been matters of deep concern to government planners. In terms of utilization, the structure of the G.D.R. population has presented some problems that are illustrated by the data in Table 2. The burden of relatively large portions of the population in "unproductive" age brackets is enormous. And projections to the year 2000 indicate only a gradual rise in the working age groups.[4]

[4] Kurt Witthauer, "Bemerkungen zur Volkszählung 1964 in der Deutschen Demokratischen Republik," *Petermanns Geographische Mitteilungen,* MIX, no. 4 (1965), 302-4.

State policies have restrained the utilization of the younger and older groups in the labor force. Youngsters are kept in school until the age of sixteen or seventeen by the mandatory ten-year polytechnical school system. To make some use of pupils in their later school years, periods of "practice" in industry or on collective farms have been worked into the curriculum. At the upper end of the age scale the state has little room to maneuver, since retirement benefits—already quite low—cannot be changed without political risk. It is easier for the state to make use of women in the labor force.[5] This includes not only the surplus population of women over thirty-three, but also young working mothers who place their children in state nurseries. (Table 3 gives an overview of the importance of women in the East German economy.)

East Germany is one of the few countries in which the population has declined since 1945. Between the censuses of 1950 and 1964, the population of the G.D.R. declined from 18,388,172 to 17,011,931—a loss of 1,376,241.[6] The principal reason for the decline in population through 1961 was the exodus to the West. The most generally cited western-movement statistic for the period 1949 through 1962 is 2,759,922.[7] This figure is less than the total number of individuals who left the G.D.R., since it represents only those who were officially registered by the Federal Republic. Not all refugees submitted to the registration process. An analysis of those registering as refugees shows that roughly

[5]See: Christine Kulke, "Die Qualifizierung der Frauen in der industriellen Produktion: Zum Problem der Frauenarbeit in der DDR," *Studien und Materialien zur Soziologie der DDR,* ed. P. C. Ludz (Köln and Opladen: Westdeutscher Verlag, 1964), pp. 145-68.

[6]*Statistisches Jahrbuch der DDR 1966,* p. 4.

[7]*SBZ von A-Z* (Bonn: Deutscher Bundesverlag, 1963), p. 147.

half were in the productive age groups, people whom the G.D.R. could not afford to lose.[8] It was this loss of vital population that was ultimately responsible for the closing of the Berlin sector boundary on August 13, 1961. Since that action the population of the G.D.R. has slowly begun to increase.

Prior to 1964 population statistics for the G.D.R. were based on projections from the censuses of October, 1946, and August, 1950. In 1957 the East German authorities announced a census to be carried out in January, 1959.[9] The purpose of the count was to provide accurate figures for a planned economy, yet it was clear that there was also a strongly political element to the census taking. The unsatisfactory outcome of a pretest that ultimately aborted the 1959 census was explained in largely ideological terms: "the staff of the State Central Administration for Statistics did not understand [the need] to work closely and collegially with the party of the workers and the mass organizations in mobilizing all resources for the success of the sample count." [10] The questionnaire overtaxed the ideological sophistication of the respondents and its technical complexity virtually guaranteed failure.

The first "socialist" census in the G.D.R. was not taken until December 31, 1964. The preliminary results indicate a 1964 population of 17,011,931—235,258

[8]Heinz Kabermann, *Die Bevölkerung des sowjetischen Besatzungsgebietes—Bestands– und Strukturveränderungen 1950-1957* (Bonn and Berlin: Bundesministerium für Gesamtdeutsche Fragen, 1961), pp. 59-60.

[9]"Gesetz über die Volks-, Berufs- und Wohnraumzählung beschlossen," *Statistische Praxis,* XIII, no. 1 (January, 1958), 2.

[10]"Erfahrungen aus der Probezählung am 20. Februar 1958 im Landkreis Leipzig," *Statistische Praxis,* XIII, no. 5 (May, 1958), 100-5.

below what the statisticians had projected for January 1, 1965 from the 1950 data.[11]

The distribution of the East German population follows the pattern of industrialization, with the greatest density in East Berlin and the area to the south, including the districts of Halle, Karl-Marx-Stadt (Chemnitz), Leipzig, and Dresden. (Table 4 shows the 1965 pattern of population distribution by districts. In order to provide a more detailed picture, Table 5 indicates population changes in some of the major cities of the G.D.R., and Table 6 describes the pattern of increasing urbanization in East Germany.)

In summary, the demographic problem of the G.D.R. after the Wall are those of a modern industrial state. The losses of the war and emigration have kept the official policy toward abortion more conservative than in the rest of the bloc partners.[12] However, the long-range prospects point to "normalization" of the demographic structure by the turn of the century.

Ethnic and language groups. The Sorbs are the only ethnic minority in the G.D.R. Their presence has given the East German leadership an opportunity to demonstrate loyalty to and appreciation of the slavic cultures with which closer relations would be sought as a matter of policy. In addition the Sorbic presence gave Walter Ulbricht yet another opportunity to emulate Josef

[11]U.S. Bureau of the Census, *Projections of the Population of the Communist Countries of Eastern Europe, by Age and Sex: 1965-1985,* by James L. Scott, International Population Reports, Series P-91, no. 14 (Washington, D.C.: U.S. Government Printing Office, 1965), p. 25.

[12]"Untersuchung über Kinderfreudigkeit," *SBZ-Archiv,* XVII, no. 12 (June, 1966), 178-79.

Stalin—in this case by following his lead in the nationalities question.

The Sorbs have maintained their own culture and language in the area around Bautzen and Hoyerswerda near the Czech-Polish frontier. In 1925 there were approximately 62,000 Sorbs in the German Reich; however, during the nazi period they were persecuted and employed as forced laborers.[13] With great tenacity the Sorbs persisted in continuing their culture and somehow had to be accommodated by the developing communist system of the G.D.R. In 1948 the *Land* government of Saxony passed the Law for the Protection of the Rights of the Sorbic Population, guaranteeing Sorbic elementary and secondary schools, making Sorbic the official language of the local bureaucracy, and establishing the Office for Sorbic Culture.[14] Later, provisions for the bilingual publication of laws and ordinances were made, and bilingual street signs appeared along with other appurtenances of cultural recognition. Article Eleven of the G.D.R. Constitution appeared to have been effected:

Article 11: The free development of the national characteristics of the foreign-language national groups in the Republic shall be encouraged by legislation and by the administration; in particular they may not be hindered in the use of their mother tongue in education, in the administration and in the courts of law.[15]

[13]Hans Lindemann, "Die Sorben in der 'DDR,'" *SBZ-Archiv*, XI, no. 15 (August, 1960), 230.
[14]Lieselotte Kramer-Kaske, "Einst Menschen zweiten Ranges. Zehn Jahre Gesetz zur Wahrung der Rechte der sorbischen Bevölkerung," *Sonntag*, XIII, no. 12 (March 23, 1958), 11 ff.
[15]*Constitution of the German Democratic Republic* (East Berlin: VEB Deutscher Zentralverlag, 1962), p. 21.

Official policy toward the Sorbic minority was ambivalent since the Sorbic outlook and attitude toward land ownership was not in harmony with the aims of the SED. On the other side, however, was the authority of Stalin's policy regarding cultural autonomy and recognition. Not surprisingly, the Stalinist interpretation prevailed. By 1952 the SED was even considering a plan to clear the Sorbic area of Germans to achieve a purely Sorbic population. Neither the Sorbs nor the Germans of the Upper and Lower Lausitz were enthusiastic about this plan and the idea was dropped.[16]

The closeness of the Sorbs to the Czech and Polish borders, in addition to the Slavic propensities of their language and culture, led the Sorbs to seek contacts in those countries. During the events of 1956, the Sorbic communists appear to have considered removing themselves from the control of the SED and joining the United Polish Workers' Party to escape the control of the German Stalinists who were threatening to smother them. The moves made by Ulbricht against revisionist elements in the SED put an end to such notions.

The only other nation displaying an interest in the Sorbs was Yugoslavia. During the Tito-Stalin split it was discovered that the Sorbs and the Serbs had much in common. After the resumption of relations between Yugoslavia and the G.D.R. in 1957, the mutual interests of the Sorbs and Serbs were nurtured to the displeasure of the SED, which characteristically noted deficiencies in party work in the Sorbic area and ordered intensified ideological activity.[17] The leader of SED activities among the Sorbs has been Kurt Krenz, a prewar communist who became head of the Domowina—the union

[16]Lindemann, "Die Sorben," p. 231.
[17]*Ibid.*, pp. 231-32.

of the Sorbs that has represented their interests since its founding in 1912.[18]

Although no reliable figures are available, it appears that in spite of special laws, schools, literature, and the Institute for Research of the Sorbic People of the German Academy of Sciences in Berlin, the number of Sorbs has declined to about 38,000.[19] Industrialization and collectivization in the Sorbic area indicate their eventual integration into the German majority, although a recent issue of *Neue Deutsche Literatur,* official publication of the East German *Schriftsteller- verband* ("authors' league"), was devoted to new Sorbic literature.[20]

Religious groups. In the pre-entry period communist policy aimed at uniting all groups in a Democratic Antifascist Order. Religious groups were no exception. A statement signed by the then co-chairmen of the SED, Wilhelm Pieck and Otto Grotewohl, dated August 27, 1946, is indicative of the party policy on the Christian churches:

Willfully determined, after the most fearsome catastrophe that the German people have suffered in their history, to construct a new, democratic Germany, the anti-fascist democratic parties combined in a United Front shortly after the collapse. Above the divisive character of their *Weltanschauungen* they [the parties] have placed the uniting element, *responsibility to the future.* The churches of

[18]*SBZ-Biographie* (Bonn and Berlin: Bundesministerium für Gesamtdeutsche Fragen, 1964), p. 195.
[19]*SBZ von A-Z* (1963), p. 522.
[20]"Heimat DDR. Neue Sorbische Epik, Dramatik, Lyrik als Bestandteile unserer sozialistischen Literatur," *Neue Deutsche Literatur,* XV, no. 3 (March, 1967).

all confessions have their part in the reconstruction of Germany.

. . . .

The Socialist Unity Party of Germany has proven its initiative and honest will in this common reconstruction work. The party has declared, to the Church, its preparedness and willingness to do everything possible to aid the confessional communities in positive cooperation in the reconstruction of Germany.[21]

The rest of the document is critical of the Christian Democratic leadership in the Soviet Zone for allegedly introducing the issue of Marxism contra Christianity. The SED declared this a challenge it would not accept: religious belief is a matter of individual preference and the SED was committed to freedom of conscience in matters of belief. In fact, so the statement continues, many Christians, laymen and clergy, have found their way to socialism because of their personal belief in Christianity. The statement concludes: "The issue is not a question of battle, *Christianity or Marxism,* but rather one of common responsibility for the future of Germany, which stands in full greatness before *Christianity and Marxism.*"[22]

East Germany is the only predominantly Protestant communist party state of the East European bloc. In 1946—14,132,174 or 81.6 per cent of the total population were members of the Evangelical (Protestant) churches; the Catholic church had 2,110,507 members or 12.2 per cent of the population at the same time.[23]

[21]Wilhelm Pieck and Otto Grotewohl, "SED und Christentum," *Dokumente der Sozialistischen Einheitspartei Deutschlands* (East Berlin: Dietz Verlag, 1948), II, 80.

[22]*Ibid.,* p. 82.

[23]Kurt Hutten, *Christen hinter dem eisernen Vorhang* (Stuttgart: Quell-Verlag, 1963), pp. 26-27.

As with most census data on religion, these figures are probably inflated. However, the proportions are approximately correct, with perhaps a larger number of Catholics as a result of the influx of refugees and expellees from Catholic areas of East Europe. During the pre-entry period there were occasional conflicts between the Christian churches and the SED, but they were not the result of antichurch campaigns that came later.

Belief System

The belief system in East Germany during the pre-entry period was relatively uniform in the period immediately following the capitulation in May, 1945. However, a trend toward increasing conflict among values and beliefs became apparent during the late 1940s.

Basic values and goals. In spite of the magnitude of the catastrophe the Germans faced on May 8, 1945, political life continued. The most basic and elemental goal in the months following surrender was physical survival. There were those, however, whose energy levels and interests were of such an order that they sought contact with others to form groups and, ultimately, political parties. The parties emerged with the permission of the authority that also controlled the means of communications and the food supply.[24]

In spite of the control that the occupying powers and their agents exercised—directly and indirectly—the various groups that began articulating the values cur-

[24]J. P. Nettl, *The Eastern Zone and Soviet Policy in Germany 1945-50* (London: Oxford University Press, 1951), pp. 100-1.

rent in Germany after the collapse were diverse in composition and Weltanschauung. From the concentration camps came communist and Social Democratic survivors of persecution who bore their own unique badge of legitimacy. The old Center Party formed part of the nucleus of a new middle-class Christian (Protestant and Catholic) party, the Christian Democratic Union (CDU). The nationalistic right and the more than routinely compromised members of the Nazi Party disappeared, at least temporarily, from public life.

Values capable of rallying these diverse groups and subgroups were democracy and antifascism. These were also the rallying points of the KPD, which had its own notions of how the Antifascist Democratic Order was to be constructed. With the backing of the Soviet Military Administration in Germany, communist leadership was gradually able to assert itself as *the* articulator of the valid and official value system for the Soviet Zone of Occupation.

The principal elements of the value system were quite simple. The nazi regime was bad. It came into being because the democratic elements of German society and politics were unable to unite in antinazi opposition. Therefore, all Germans must unite to destroy the fascist order and then construct a new, democratic Germany. As time went on, the negative basic value—the antifascist element—increasingly became an abstraction modified by the role the KPD played as "the" opponent of the rising and established nazi party of the 1920s and '30s. The positive goal of a democratic order became a democratic order in the communist sense. Finally, in 1948-49, after the division of Germany was sealed, a new Germany was to be constructed under the direction of the party of workers and peasants which would lead a co-operative effort of all progressive elements in German society regardless of their actual political ties.

The SED membership figures in 1946 and 1947 reflect efforts to distribute, and the distribution of, the values fixed to its banner. At the time of the forced merger of the SPD with the KPD (April, 1946), the new party numbered 1,298,415. In the succeeding year the SED membership rose to 1,786,138—a monthly increase of some 40,000.[25] Before the conflict between Stalin and Tito in the summer of 1948, the SED was clearly a mass party that actively sought new members. As troubles developed within the East European complex and as the Soviet Union and the other occupying powers in Germany came to an impasse (blockade of June, 1948), the SED underwent a purge aimed at changing it into a "Party of the New Type" following the model and lead of the Communist Party of the Soviet Union.

The propagation of the SED value system was aided by the approximately 150 KPD members who had undergone special schooling programs during the years of exile in the Soviet Union.[26] Educational work had also been conducted among German prisoners of war, especially after the Soviet victory at Stalingrad. In fact, a second plane full of Germans from the Soviet Union landed in Dresden one day after the "Ulbricht Group" had arrived in Frankfurt-on-the-Oder. It contained a select group of reliable functionaries familiar with the goals and methods of the KPD, some of whom had been members of the "National Committee for a Free Ger-

[25]Carola Stern, *Porträt einer Bolschewistischen Partei* (Köln: Verlag für Politik und Wirtschaft, 1957), p. 51.
[26]Leonhard, *Die Revolution*, chaps. 1-4.

many," a propaganda and political agitation organization working among German war prisoners.[27]

Expectation of goal achievement. The decisive factor in the achievement of communist expectations was the support of the Soviet Military Administration (SMAD). SMAD controlled the licensing of political parties and the allocation of paper and food. Apart from reparations activities, SMAD also ordered basic changes in the economic organization of its zone of occupation.[28] This backing in the drive for the construction of a democratic order of the "socialist" variety rendered the expectations and values of other-minded individuals and groups in the Soviet Zone largely irrelevant by the end of the pre-entry period.

Cultural orientation. Situated in the center of Europe, Germany has been ambivalent in its cultural orientation between the West, as symbolized by France, and the East, which has been characterized by a more complex set of relationships ranging from colonization and expansionism to the "romantic" affinities felt by some poets and literary figures for Slavic culture. In a sense the present existence of "East" and "West" Germanys is ironically symbolic of the part Germany has played as an intermediary looking both East and West and mediating intellectually, culturally, religiously, and sometimes politically.[29]

[27]Stern, *Porträt,* pp. 12-13.
[28]See, for example: SMAD Orders No. 64 and No. 76, *Zentralverordnungsblatt—Jahrgang 1948,* pp. 140–45. These orders ended the sequestration of nazi and "capitalist" properties, directing their conversion into publicly owned enterprises.
[29]H. H. Bielfeldt, ed., *Deutsch-Slawische Wechselseitigkeit in sieben Jahrhunderten* (East Berlin: Akademie-Verlag, 1956).

In the pre-entry period the direction of the cultural orientation of the Soviet Zone, from an official perspective, was eastward toward the Soviet Union. This can be seen in the treatment of philosophy and history in the universities of the Soviet Zone. In reopening the University of Jena in October, 1945, the responsible Red Army officer wished the faculty well in its efforts to overcome the fascist past and to construct democracy in Germany.[30] However, no lectures in philosophy and history were allowed until the winter semester 1946-47. During this period compromised philosophers were removed from faculties. Those remaining were subject to close scrutiny, particularly after the resumption of lectures. Scrutiny took the form of lengthy reports to Soviet officials concerning personal philosophical views and the monitoring of lectures.[31]

On the more positive side, the emerging orientation was aided by the establishment of lectureships in dialectical and historical materialism. The Soviet and German communist officials were aware that they would not be able to change the outlook of most of the professors; therefore they concentrated on controlling the ideological orientation of students in special study groups that became mandatory parts of university curricula, designed to introduce and reinforce Marxism-Leninism.[32] As a result of these added strictures thir-

[30]"Die Philosophie in der Sowjetzone," *Der Monat,* II, no. 21 (June, 1950), 251.

[31]*Ibid.,* pp. 250-55. See also: Bernd Kaltenbach, *Die Fachrichtung Philosophie an den Universitäten der Sowjetzone 1945-1958* (Bonn and Berlin: Bundesministerium für Gesamtdeutsche Fragen, 1960), chap. 1; and M. G. Lange, *Wissenschaft im totalitären Staat* (Stuttgart and Düsseldorf: Ring-Verlag, 1955), chaps. 1-3.

[32]Egon and Marianne Müller, ". . . *stürmt die Festung Wissenschaft!"* (Berlin-Dahlem: Colloquium-Verlag, 1953), pt. I.

teen clearly noncompromised professors of philosophy left the Soviet Zone between 1945 and 1950.[33] Their departure helped clear the field for socialist reconstruction.

The cultural orientation toward the Soviet Union was further increased by placing emphasis on the teaching of the Russian language at all levels of the school system. Through required courses in Russian, "the influence of Russian and of the political jargon of communism has been considerable." [34] The Soviet trend was also manifested in school study plans for history. In 1947 the Russian October Revolution was granted four hours in the study guide; by 1950 the Revolution and its consequences took up sixteen hours.[35]

The impact of the official cultural orientation that developed in the pre-entry period and its relation to the belief system of the people is difficult to assess. The policies of the SMAD and the German communist leadership were clear. But the depth and extent of their influence is a matter of speculation.

Several factors worked against successful Soviet influence in this and later periods. First and foremost was the experience of the defeat in war with the Soviet Union. The difficulty the vanquished felt in embracing the victor after a total war was complicated by a second factor—years of nazi anti-Soviet propaganda (with the fleeting exception of the Hitler-Stalin pact interlude). The occupation itself was a third obstacle to Soviet success; it served as a daily reminder of defeat, reinforcing

[33]"Die Philosophie in der Sowjetzone," p. 250.
[34]John T. Waterman, *A History of the German Language* (Seattle: University of Washington Press, 1966), pp. 179-80.
[35]M. G. Lange, *Totalitäre Erziehung* (Frankfurt am Main: Verlag der Frankfurter Hefte, 1954), p. 83.

recent, overwhelmingly negative memories. Finally, the Soviet efforts at reorientation had to compete with similar activities based on a differing value and belief system in the western zones of occupied Germany. This is nowhere more clearly demonstrated than in the city of Berlin and the case of the establishment of the Free University of Berlin in 1948.[36] The introduction of intellectually numbing but mandatory courses in dialectical and historical materialism, Marxism-Leninism, and political economy, in addition to increasing political control over teachers and students, set the scene for the founding of the Free University and a lasting conflict in the G.D.R. between youth and their indoctrinators, who were identified with the Soviet Union.

Religion. The real conflicts between the SED and organized religion did not begin until after the pre-entry period had ended. Perhaps one reason for restraint was the increase in religious activity throughout Germany during the period following the surrender. Indicative of the interest in religious matters are the statistics for German book production for the year 1947: 8,612 books were registered in the *Nationalbibliographie.* Of these, 1,927 were grouped under the category *belle lettres*; religious books next, with 1,299 titles.[37] Many of these religious books were short, which meant lower prices and conceivably broader distribution than might be expected of an equal number of longer works.

The antagonistic attitude of the SED toward the Christian churches was evident in spite of relative peace

[36]Egon and Marianne Müller, ". . . *stürmt die Festung Wissenschaft!"*, pp. 116-22.
[37]*Börsenblatt für den Deutschen Buchhandel,* no. 18 (May, 1948), 168.

on the surface. Attacks on the Christian Democratic Union, which became a symbol for the Catholic church in the pronouncements of the SED, and Walter Ulbricht's "Open Answer to the Christian Democratic Union" given in October, 1946, made it clear that "it was never good for the Church when it let itself be drawn into battles between [political] parties." [38] At the same time Ulbricht made a point of the fact that Protestants and Catholics were participating in all parties, including the SED.

Nationalism. Proletarian internationalism and nationalism have been, at times, uncomfortable elements to reconcile within the whole of the communist program. During World War II the contradiction was temporarily solved in the opposition to nazi Germany. Essentially the same solution was adopted by German communists in the immediate postwar period with the added notion of "good" communist nationalism and "bad" imperialist-capitalist nationalism. The KPD program of the summer of 1945 gave its answer to the internationalism versus nationalism question:

Our national fight is the fight against reaction and imperialism, for the recognition of the equality of all peoples, for peace and for freedom. This fight is indeed that of proletarian internationalism.[39]

This line in somewhat modified forms was maintained through the Second Party Congress of the Social-

[38]Walter Ulbricht, "Offene Antwort an die Christlich-Demokratische Union," *Zur Geschichte der Deutschen Arbeiterbewegung* (East Berlin: Dietz Verlag, 1960), III, 46.

[39]Hans Müller, *Die Entwicklung der SED und ihr Kampf für ein neues Deutschland (1945-1949)* (East Berlin: Dietz Verlag, 1961), p. 79.

ist Unity Party in September, 1947. Here Otto Grotewohl said:

The leadership of the German nation can only be assumed
by the German working class, and our duty consists in
making clear the role of the working class in the coming
party discussions. The position of the working class in relation to the national question has nothing to do with nationalistic tendencies. It is nothing other than the will to
commit its entire power to the preservation of the German
people.[40]

A more clearly nationalistic chord was struck by the
SED pronouncements concerning the unification of
Germany. As early as 1946 Ulbricht pursued the line
that the western capitalists and the creators of "Bi-
Zonia" were responsible for the division of the German
nation. In responding to the Stuttgart speech of Secre-
tary Byrnes, in which a provisional German government had been suggested, Ulbricht declared:

*One cannot artificially divide a Germany that through
the centuries became a unified German Reich, unless
one wishes to make the various parts of Germany into
dominions.*[41]

The nationalist appeal was strong, but it was felt necessary to coat the land reform programs and other elements of the changing Soviet Zone economy with something that might appeal to people in the western zones.
Party declarations were backed by efforts to create a

[40]Otto Grotewohl, "Zum II. Parteitag," *Im Kampf um die
einige Deutsche Demokratische Republik* (East Berlin: Dietz
Verlag, 1959), I, 108.
[41]Walter Ulbricht, "Um die Zukunft Deutschlands," *Die Entwicklung des deutschen volksdemokratischen Staates 1945-1958*
(East Berlin: Dietz Verlag, 1959), p. 106.

new "national consciousness" through the school system. Very soon after the war efforts were made to reinterpret the history of German culture. After all, Germany was the land of Marx and Engels. Much was made of nineteenth-century German realists in art and literature. The heroes of the resistance, especially those who were communists, were held up as representative of the best in the German national tradition,[42] an appeal that was nearly impossible to resist. The nationalist appeal of the KPD/SED in the pre-entry period had a strange sound when it reverberated against the ever-present sounding board of the SMAD. Few Germans could possibly have shared Walter Ulbricht's enthusiasm when in 1945 he said: *"We are bound to be deeply thankful to the people of the Soviet Union,* because they made the greatest of sacrifices in destroying the fascist German imperialists, therewith creating the prerequisites with which the German people could at last construct a new, democratic order."* [43]

Image of self in the world. The German self-image in the world at the end of the war is still a matter of speculation. Defeat, disillusionment, and hunger led large segments of the population to withdrawal from politics, as the interest in religion might indicate. When attention is shifted to the politically relevant groups in the Soviet Zone, a somewhat clearer picture emerges. The four parties licensed by the Soviet Military Administration in 1945—the KPD, the SPD, the Liberal Demo-

[42]Lange, *Totalitäre Erziehung,* pp. 114-17; and Stern, *Porträt,* pp. 68-71.
[43]Walter Ulbricht, "Hallesche Sozialdemokraten und Kommunisten für die Einheit der Arbeiterklasse," *Die Entwicklung,* p. 41.

cratic Party of Germany (LDPD), and the Christian Democratic Union (CDU)—established, through their party programs, images with which the voting population of the Soviet Zone could identify itself, at least in the period of its relative independence prior to and at the first elections.

In the elections to the provincial legislatures of October 21, 1946, the Socialist Unity Party netted no more than 50 per cent of the vote in any single province (Mecklenburg-Pommern) in spite of its advantaged position in the competition. Zonewide, the SED polled 4,625,925 to 2,398,035 for the CDU and 2,410,146 for the LDPD.[44] In Berlin where "unfused" Social Democrats competed, the SED ran third, more than 500,000 votes behind the victorious SPD and 48,000 votes in arrears of the second place CDU.[45]

Identification with other countries. During the pre-entry period East Germany was in much the same position as the western occupation zones: Germany was a nation defeated in war and generally despised by those nations that had fought Germany and had suffered occupation by nazi forces. If it is accepted that identification ultimately requires mutuality, Germany had little to identify with outside its own borders.

Certainly Germany did not, as the pre-entry period progressed, continue to occupy the pariah position that it did after World War I. The cold war drew the eastern and western zones of occupation into something resembling the dominion status that Walter Ulbricht indicated in the speech quoted above. As Germany—East and West—became allied with the respective sys-

[44]Nettl, *The Eastern Zone,* pp. 90–92.
[45]*Ibid.,* p. 94.

tems, mutuality and aspects of integration between occupied and occupier became apparent.

A base for directing German identification with the Soviet Union was instituted with the founding in 1947 of the Society for the Study of the Culture of the Soviet Union, later called the Society for German-Soviet Friendship. The membership figures for the Society in the pre-entry period indicate that it did not achieve a mass base until after the establishment of the G.D.R. in 1949.

Indicative of the kind of work the Society did in encouraging German-Soviet understanding is this report of a public discussion between Red Army Captain Tregubov and Albert Norden, later Politbüro member of the SED:

It was not the German people who shook off its fascist masters, but the Soviet Army which had to spill its blood all the way to Berlin in order that the German worker might be free again. In view of this it is not the Soviet people who must change their attitude toward the Germans, rather it is the Germans who must change their attitudes toward the Soviet people. That is the only way that we [the Germans] shall overcome the past, create the new and again win the confidence of the peace-loving peoples.[46]

The aim of the Society has been to spread information about the Soviet Union in countless meetings, lectures, and exhibits. The work of the Society supported the newly emerging cultural orientation of East Germany.

Response patterns to crisis. Two crises in the pre-entry period showed a SED response pattern that was

[46]Hans Müller, *Die Entwicklung der SED,* p. 194.

25

to be characteristic in later crisis situations: the blockade of the land routes used by the Western occupying powers to reach Berlin, and the Stalin-Tito split of the same year, 1948.

The reaction to the East-West crisis was to turn the attention of the Soviet Zone inward. At the time of the blockade (June 24, 1948), a currency reform was introduced in the Soviet Zone. This action was part of the stress on increased productivity directed by SMAD Order 234 of October, 1947, and which continued the transition to a Soviet-style planned economy with the half-year plan of July-December, 1948. In effect the Soviet Union was shifting its German policy from one directed at the whole of Germany to one concentrating on its zone of occupation.[47]

The reaction to the crisis within the socialist camp was the transformation of the SED into a Party of the New Type, a cadre party rather than the mass party that the SED had been since its establishment in 1946. Membership was reduced and those who remained were expected to participate more fully in the work of the party and also to take part in special schools to train and retrain reinstated members. Candidate membership status was introduced. The Party of the New Type condemned those German communists—including Anton Ackermann—who had evolved theories envisioning a "German Road to Socialism." The internal parallels with the Yugoslav case were obvious and conscious.[48]

[47]*Ibid.*, p. 178; and Stern, *Porträt,* p. 78.
[48]"Für die organisatorische Festigung der Partei und für ihre Säuberung von feindlichen und entarteten Elementen," *Dokumente der Sozialistischen Einheitspartei Deutschlands,* II, 78-83; Hans Müller, *Die Entwicklung der SED,* pp. 191-93; and Stern, *Porträt,* pp. 85-90.

Social System

Agricultural. Two measures effected in the year after the German surrender had a profound impact on the East German social system—an impact that was to be reinforced throughout later periods. The first measure was the agrarian land reform carried out in 1945 and early 1946; the second was the reform of the school system.

Land reform was high on the list of the KPD policy priorities. From the Soviet Union the KPD leaders brought with them a clear picture of the great problems that faced a "socialist" transformation of agriculture. They also harbored a deep dislike for the large landholders, which was reinforced by the intensely negative affect the term *Junker* had acquired—not only among communists but also among other sectors of the population as well. These considerations combined to give a grim determination to efforts in the agrarian sector.

The major action was carried out in September, 1945, in all of the agricultural areas of the Soviet Zone.[49] All farms over 100 hectares were taken from their owners, as were all agricultural establishments belonging to people classified as war criminals and nazis. Some 500 larger farms were transformed into People's Farms that were later to become models for agricultural collectives. The great majority of the land, however, was distributed as follows:

> 7,112 farms of over 100 hectares totaling 2,500,000 hectares were taken from private ownership;

[49]Hans Müller, *Die Entwicklung der SED,* pp. 55-62.

27

4,278 farms of less than 100 hectares totaling 124,000 hectares were taken from private ownership;

with other lands a total of 3,220,000 hectares was made available for redistribution.

This acreage was divided among:

119,530 landless peasants and agricultural workers who received 924,365 hectares;

89,529 expellees who received 754,976 hectares;

80,404 peasants with insufficient land who received 270,949 hectares.

The rest went to small tenants, workers, established peasantry, and People's Farms.[50]

The proliferation of small ownerships was not consistent with the ends of communist ideology, but it did correspond as a developmental phase with the New Economic Policy in the Soviet Union.[51] The reform effectively and radically eliminated a segment of society, replacing it with a restructured agrarian population.

Educational. The school reform of the pre-entry period was motivated by a desire to change the heritage of the past and to create conditions conducive to a socialist future. One element of this drive was directed at eliminating politically compromised teachers. This was not always an easy task in view of the influx of individuals from the East about whom little was known,

[50]Summary figures from *SBZ von A-Z* (1963), p. 87.

[51]Willi Wapenhans, "Ueber das Wesen der landwirtschaftlichen Produktionsgenossenschaften in Mitteldeutschland," *Zeitschrift für das gesamte Genossenschaftswesen,* II, no. 1 (1961), 3-4.

added to the fact that radical elimination of all persons with a politically questionable past would have led to a severe shortage of teachers.

A second element of the school reform was directed toward creating a unified school system that would "guarantee all youth, boys and girls, urban and rural without regard to the wealth of their parents, an equal right to an education and its achievement consistent with aptitudes and abilities." [52]

Traditionally German higher education had been the preserve of the middle and upper classes.[53] Volksschulen were made available to those not destined for higher education, mainly the children of working-class parents. The unified school was designed to overcome this division.[54] Church-sponsored schools were eliminated; Workers' and Peasants' Faculties were added to the universities to provide an avenue to higher education for those lacking the standard preparatory course. The organization of the East German educational system was revised in subsequent periods, always with a view to the effects that education might have on the social system.

Political. In the pre-entry period the basic political system of the future G.D.R. took form. The major fact

[52]Lange, *Totalitäre Erziehung,* p. 40. The citation is from the Law Concerning the Democratization of the German Schools. For school policies in this period see: *Ibid.,* chap. 2. An English treatment can be found in Paul S. Bodenman, *Education in the Soviet Zone of Germany* (Washington, D.C.: U.S. Government Printing Office, 1959).

[53]For a recent discussion with comparisons see: Ralf Dahrendorf, "Arbeiterkinder an unseren Universitäten," *Die Zeit* (North American Edition), no. 25 (June 26, 1964), p. 10, and no. 26 (July 3, 1964), p. 10.

[54]Hans Müller, *Die Entwicklung der SED,* pp. 62-65.

of political life was the presence of the Soviet occupation and its special relationship with the KPD/SED. This made Soviet policy a matter of crucial importance, as the watershed year 1948 clearly shows. Before the Berlin blockade and the Stalin-Tito split, political activity was freer than after the summer of 1948, when the SED became a Party of the New Type, brooking less and less deviation from its established line.

The "pluralism" of the 1945-48 period involved four (later three) parties: KPD, SPD, LDPD, and CDU. The first two parties became the Socialist Unity Party (SED). But even before the forced unification of the KPD and SPD, rather stringent limits were set on the range of pluralism by the bloc of the Antifascist Democratic Parties, established shortly after SMAD licensed the parties in the summer of 1945. With the backing of SMAD, the communists clearly assumed the leadership role within the Bloc and looked upon the other parties as representatives of particular interest groups within Soviet Zone society. The bourgeoisie was represented by the LDPD [55] and the CDU—to which was added the National Democratic Party of Germany (NDPD) in 1948. In the same year the Democratic Peasants' Federation of Germany (DBD) was founded to represent the interests of the "working peasant." [56]

This interest representation extended to the mass organizations of the Soviet Zone which were established and led by SED members who set their policies.[57] The

[55]For a treatment of the LDPD in this period see: E. Krippendorff, *Die Liberal-Demokratische Partei Deutschlands in der Sowjetischen Besatzungszone 1945/48* (Düsseldorf: Droste Verlag, n.d.).

[56]Ernst Richert, *Macht ohne Mandat* (Köln and Opladen: Westdeutscher Verlag, 1958), pp. 113-14.

[57]For the role of the SED in the mass organizations see: Hans Müller, *Die Entwicklung der SED,* pp. 138-48.

mass organizations represented labor (Free German Trade Union Federation—FDGB), women (Democratic Womens Federation—DFD), peasants (Peasants Mutual Aid Union—VDGB), youth (Free German Youth—FDJ), and intellectuals (German Cultural Federation—DK). Since these mass organizations were represented in the legislature of the G.D.R., they were able to obtain certain advantages for their respective groups in exchange for complete and active support of the SED line.[58]

Economic. In the pre-entry period the foundations were laid for a planned economy based on the Soviet model. SMAD Order No. 138, dated June 27, 1947, established the first central agency in the German administration in the Soviet Zone of Occupation—the *Deutsche Wirtschaftskommission* (German Economic Commission).[59] The Economic Commission, which was to become the nucleus of the G.D.R. government, was the central German agency for industry, finance, transport, trade, supply, labor, agriculture and forestry, energy, interzonal and foreign trade, and statistics.[60] Other central administrations acted together with the Economic Commission, but without an office or an individual in a central position to co-ordinate all activities.

Order No. 32 of SMAD, dated February 12, 1948, broadened the powers of the Economic Commission "in order to draw the German democratic executive agencies into active participation in the reconstruction and

[58]Richert, *Macht ohne Mandat,* pp. 114-15.
[59]The German Central Administration for Public Education was instituted on a zonewide basis before the Economic Commission, but had nowhere near the authority of the latter.
[60]*SBZ von A-Z* (1962), p. 104.

development of a peace economy in the Soviet Zone of Occupation." The central administrations (Interior, Justice, Health, and Public Education), the zonal labor organization and farmers' organization were given representation on the Economic Commission headed by Heinrich Rau and two deputies: Bruno Leuschner and Fritz Selbmann—names that were to figure prominently in East German economic planning for over twelve years.[61]

[61]Heinrich Rau was born the son of a farmer in 1899 and was Minister for Foreign and Domestic Trade in 1961. His biography is that of a model communist functionary. He was a member of the Independent Social Democratic Party and the Communist Party of Germany (from 1919 on) before World War II. Imprisoned by the nazis in 1933, he emigrated to Czechoslovakia upon release. Later he took part in the Spanish Civil War in the Eleventh International Brigade. He was arrested in France in 1939 and turned over to the Gestapo, which imprisoned him in the concentration camp Mauthausen. After the war he rejoined the Communist Party and has occupied top positions in the SED ever since. Rau has twelve decorations, including one each from North Korea and the U.A.R.

Bruno Leuschner was born in 1910, the son of a shoemaker. Leuschner joined the Communist Party in 1931 and spent the years between 1936 and 1945 imprisoned in various concentration camps. From 1947 to 1961 he was responsible for central planning in the G.D.R., serving as head of the State Planning Commission from 1952 to 1961. After 1961 Leuschner was Deputy Chairman of the Council of Ministers, responsible for basic economic co-ordination. Leuschner died on February 10, 1965.

Fritz Selbmann is the same age as Rau and is of working-class background. Selbmann has been active in the communist movement since 1922. He was imprisoned during most of the nazi era. From 1955 to 1958 he was Deputy Chairman of the Council of Ministers and from 1958 to 1961 he was Deputy Chairman of the State Planning Commission; he has also held other important positions in the economic bureaucracy. In his party career Selbmann has had difficulties because of his pragmatic rather than programmatic approach to economic development.

Biographical data from *SBZ-Biographie* and Stern, *Porträt,* pp. 297-334.

Before the SED party conference in July, 1948, Walter Ulbricht outlined the scope of the powers of the Economic Commission:

Order 32 of the SMAD transferred to the German Economic Commission, as the central German agency, the political and therewith the legislative and administrative responsibility for economic construction measures.

The German Economic Commission is for this reason the highest economic administrative organization upon which is incumbent administrative control in carrying out the [Two-Year] Plan. The dispositions, orders and resolutions of the German Economic Commission are binding on all governmental and administrative departments in the Soviet Zone of Occupation, as well as on all citizens. That means that the Two-Year-Plan that has been accepted as a working basis for the German Economic Commission, has become the legal working basis for the entire Zone and thus, that work immediately based on this Plan must begin.[62]

In the text of Order 32 the working relationship between the Soviet administration and the Economic Commission was emphasized:

In carrying out the objectives mentioned [see above] the Economic Commission will be given the power to draw up, issue, and control the carrying out of directives and instructions that are, in harmony with the order of the SMAD, binding on all German departments in the area of the Soviet Zone of Occupation in Germany.[63]

[62]Walter Ulbricht, "Die gegenwärtigen Aufgaben der demokratischen Verwaltung," *Die Entwicklung*, pp. 131-32.

[63]Paragraph 4, SMAD Order No. 32 (February 12, 1948) cited in: Gustav Leissner, *Verwaltung und öffentlicher Dienst in der sowjetischen Besatzungszone Deutschlands* (Stuttgart and Köln: Kohlhammer Verlag, 1961), p. 276.

The first major task of the Economic Commission was the co-ordination of reparations payments to the Soviet Union. Section three of Order 32 stated:

The Economic Commission is obliged to carry out on schedule the delivery of goods defined as reparations as well as to oversee the fulfillment of the needs of the Soviet forces of occupation in Germany according to the plan agreed upon.[64]

During 1948 the Economic Commission was expanded by the addition of People's Representatives and representatives of mass organizations and political parties, the move being based on Soviet Military Administration Order No. 183, dated November 27, 1948. Eleven months later the Economic Commission and its secretariat became the Provisional Government of the G.D.R.

East Germany as a Self-Fulfilling Unit

It is difficult to speak of East Germany as a self-fulfilling unit in the pre-entry period for two reasons. First, the economic base was radically changed by the boundary that cut off the Zone from its traditional sources of raw materials. This meant that a new base for economic self-fulfillment had to be found. The second reason that makes it difficult to speak of self-fulfillment in this period is the reparations program in the Soviet Zone which was made to pay for all Germany.[65] Western estimates of reparations payments were about 25

[64]*Ibid.*, p. 12.
[65]Ruth Fischer, *Die Umformung der Sowjetgesellschaft* (Düsseldorf and Köln: Eugen Diederichs Verlag, 1958), p. 91.

per cent of current production in the seven years following the war.[66] A figure of 26.5 billion dollars is given as the total reparations payment from 1945 through 1953.[67] Most of this payment was made in the first years after the war in the form of factories carried off to the Soviet Union. In addition Soviet Stock Corporations were established in the G.D.R. which produced almost exclusively for Soviet consumption.[68] A graphic and detailed account from the Soviet side can be found in *Soviet Economic Policy in Postwar Germany*.[69] All of this meant that the possibilities for economic self-fulfillment were restricted.

At the time of the transition of the Soviet Zone to the G.D.R., there was an indication of sociopolitical self-fulfillment in the basic negative value of antifascism. As part of an effort to encompass all elements of society, the National Democratic Party of Germany which sought the support of former nazis and professional soldiers had been licensed by the SMAD in June, 1948.[70] The effort to integrate these people into the Soviet zonal society culminated in the mass pardon in the fall of 1949, a pardon granted by the Provisional Government of the German Democratic Republic.

Walter Ulbricht's speech justifying the pardon deserves some attention, for it sheds light on the official

[66]Wolfgang Stolper, *The Structure of the East German Economy* (Cambridge, Mass.: Harvard University Press, 1960), p. 5; and Walter Ulbricht, *Zur sozialistischen Entwicklung der Volkswirtschaft seit 1945* (East Berlin: Dietz Verlag, 1959), p. 162.

[67]*SBZ von A-Z* (1963), p. 404.

[68]Walter Ulbricht, "Brennende Fragen des Neuaufbaus Deutschlands," *Zur Sozialistischen Entwicklung*, pp. 81-82.

[69]Robert Slusser, ed., *Soviet Economic Policy in Postwar Germany* (New York: Research Program on the U.S.S.R., 1953).

[70]Wolfgang Treue, *Die deutschen Parteien* (Wiesbaden: Franz Steiner Verlag, 1961), p. 60.

interpretation of the fulfillment of the antinazi value and also the democratic goal. Denazification was spoken of in the past tense: denazification and demilitarization were both accomplished, at least officially. This then made it possible to restore the rights of citizenship to former members of the Nazi Party and former Wehrmacht officers. The government was motivated to carry through the pardon because of the many former nazis and officers who had taken part in the democratic reconstruction of Germany. After giving several examples of model former nazis, Ulbricht went on to say that these people ought to be allowed full participation in all aspects of society with the exception of internal administration and the field of justice "because these organs of the state have the special duty to protect our Democracy from saboteurs and destructive elements." Ulbricht's speech ended with a call to active participation in the construction of a new Germany.[71]

No reliable statistics on East German denazification are available, making it difficult to assess the extent of the program. It would seem that an individual's past counted inversely to his willingness to participate to the full in whatever the state desired. Only to that extent can one speak of a measure of self-fulfillment in this area. Indeed, it is often difficult to distinguish between the prosecution of nazis and those accused of antistate activity.[72]

[71]Walter Ulbricht, "Begründung zum Gesetz über den Erlass von Sühnemassnahmen und die Gewährung staatsbürgerlicher Rechte für ehemalige Mitglieder und Anhänger der Nazipartei und Offiziere der faschistischen Wehrmacht," *Die Entwicklung*, pp. 180-83; and Ulbricht, "Zur Auflösung der Entnazifizierungskommissionen," *Zur Geschichte*, III, 195-98.

[72]Karl Wilhelm Fricke, "Bilanz der politischen Verfolgung seit 1945," *SBZ-Archiv*, XVI, no. 7 (April, 1965), 98-102.

Degree of Integration with Other Systems

The pre-entry period cannot be described in terms of integration in the strict sense. Germany was a defeated and occupied country, whose relations with other nations were carried out either by or through the occupying powers. Although limited, there were some pre-integrative elements in the pre-entry situation of the Soviet Zone. These are to be found in the Soviet Union-Soviet Zone relationship and in early approaches made by the SED to its East European neighbors.

Some mention has been made of the reparations made by the Soviet Zone to the Soviet Union and of the measures that the SMAD undertook to begin the conversion of the Soviet Zone into what might be termed "Soviet Germany." The Soviet Union made use of the pre-integrative element of the reparations complex in its first postwar Five Year Plan (1946-50).[73] Furthermore, the SMAD could and did use its influence over economic development to direct the reconstruction of the East German economy in accord with Soviet plan needs.

Although the overwhelming direction of the influence was from the Soviet Union to the Soviet Zone, there were a few tendencies in the other direction. Among these was the probable influence of the German scientists and technicians who were removed to the Soviet Union after the war or who were drawn from the ranks of the German war prisoners. There are no data for measuring the effect that these Germans had

[73]Konstantin Pritzel, *Die wirtschaftliche Integration der sowjetischen Besatzungszone Deutschlands in den Ostblock und ihre politische Aspekte* (Bonn and Berlin: Bundesministerium für Gesamtdeutsche Fragen, 1962), p. 18.

on certain segments of Soviet life, but their presence should be noted.[74]

The industries that were dismantled and resurrected in the Soviet Union also had some effect on the Soviet economy and on Soviet technology. In several cases the German plants were more advanced than equivalent Soviet installations, enabling the economies of the two areas to move a bit closer to each other through technological adjustments. The extent of the effect cannot be measured, especially since maximum use was not made of the dismantled plants, which were in some cases left to rust on railroad sidings or which simply could not be utilized effectively.

Although the German communists made an effort to indicate their influence on the SMAD,[75] there is little likelihood that they shared in the decision-making process even in such "integrated" sectors as the uranium mining industry, which was founded almost immediately after the war and continues to supply the Soviet Union through a Soviet stock corporation, Wismut AG.[76] The G.D.R. share in decision making increased later, not primarily as a result of formal independence, but rather through its increasing economic prominence as the most important trading partner of the U.S.S.R. in the Soviet Bloc.

Compatibility of Demands Relevant to Integration

Germany's position after the war did not make her relationships with former enemy-nations easy. None-

[74]A. M. Hanhardt, Jr., "The *Deutsche Akademie der Wissenschaften zu Berlin* and the Organization of Research in East Germany" (Ph.D. diss., Northwestern University, 1963), p. 65.
[75]Ulbricht, "Brennende Fragen," p. 81.
[76]Schmidt-Renner, *Wirtschaftsterritorium,* p. 89.

theless, some progress was made in international relations during the pre-entry period. Officially there was a desire for closer contacts with other nations. And since the controlling elite of East Germany was communist and had the support of the SMAD, the eastward direction of the slowly developing contacts was definitively established.

The East German political elite was made up largely of the leadership group of the KPD/SED supported by the SMAD. This group, consisting of communists and some Social Democrats, served as a basis for co-operation between and among the various national communist parties, within the tradition of socialist and communist internationalism.

The international tradition of the communist movement formed the core of the East German elite's definitive statements on the problem of international relations. Otto Grotewohl, speaking on the theme "Friendship with all Peoples" in August, 1947, declared that since nazism had been eradicated on the east side of the zonal boundary, the basis for trusting relations between Germany and other nations had been established. As examples of this trust and the resurgence of international relations, Grotewohl indicated that exchanges of persons had taken place: a Free German Youth delegation marched in a sport parade in Moscow and student groups had established contact with counterparts in other lands.[77] The sparseness of these examples speaks for itself.

The difficulties in restoring international contacts are exemplified by the scientific community. The official statements of the German Academy of Sciences in

[77]Otto Grotewohl, "Freundschaft mit allen Völkern," *Im Kampf*, I, 91-95.

Berlin indicated that international contacts, vital to the progress of science, were only slowly being restored after 1945. Formal international contacts were carried on through the SMAD and a few international scientific commissions.[78]

The potential benefits of integration during the preentry period were manifest in the East German economic situation. Without raw materials the economy of the Soviet Zone could not function. Because sufficient raw materials could only be obtained through international trade, considerable foreign trade efforts had to be launched.

In the summer of 1948 Walter Ulbricht could report to the SED that trade talks had been carried on with Hungary, Poland, Czechoslovakia, Rumania, and Bulgaria. The structure of foreign trade in 1947 had shown a shortage of raw materials in the economy: 89.2 per cent of the imports were raw materials, whereas only 17.6 per cent of the exports were in that class.[79] The same report indicated the direction of trade relations toward the People's Democracies. The statement that Western trade would not be neglected was gratuitous, as shown by early efforts to free the Soviet Zone from economic dependence upon Western sources.[80]

Given the international political configuration of 1948 and after, the costs of nonintegration were much higher than those of integration. Since the Soviet occupation in a sense "predetermined" the direction of the Soviet Zone, it remained for the political control

[78]Hanhardt, "The *Deutsche Akademie*," p. 66.
[79]Walter Ulbricht, "Der Zweijahrplan zur Wiederherstellung und Entwicklung der Friedenswirtschaft," *Zur sozialistischen Entwicklung,* pp. 134-36.
[80]Hans Müller, *Die Entwicklung der SED,* p. 179.

groups—the SED, the licensed parties, and mass organizations—to attempt to generate, for the society at large, a positive attitude toward the new integration.

Given the years of nazi propaganda against the Soviet Union and "the Slavs," the outcome of the war, the conduct of Red Army troops, and the presence of expellees and refugees from East Europe, it seems reasonable to assume that the idea of identifying with the Soviet Union and the nations from the Baltic through the Balkans had limited appeal. In spite of the enthusiasm expressed by the communist political elite, the population generally looked eastward with some distaste—a feeling reinforced by mutuality and the memories of soldiers and prisoners of war who had experienced the eastern front.

During the pre-entry period the communist leadership tried to pave the way for future identification by taking actions calculated to evoke mutual trust among the nations with whom the East Germans had to trade in securing a new economic base. The negative side of this effort was calculated to disengage the Soviet Zone from the West both economically and culturally, especially after the summer of 1948.

Of all the countries neighboring East Germany the most difficult with which to achieve any degree of identification, quite apart from integration, was, and remains, Poland—which symbolizes the problems of German relations within the communist system. In October, 1948, Walter Ulbricht issued a report on the results of a visit of SED leaders in Poland which emphasized two points: first, the Oder-Neisse boundary was considered a "peace boundary" between Germany and Poland; second, the Polish people were not to be looked upon as inferior—as nazi propaganda had portrayed them. Indeed, since the Poles were further advanced along the road to socialism than the Germans, they ought to be viewed as an example to follow. Ulbricht summed up the situation by saying: "The population of the Soviet Zone of Occupation must decide where it wants to go. One cannot expect to receive foodstuffs and raw materials from the Soviet Union and the People's Democracies while at the same time pursuing an anti-Soviet and nationalist propaganda against these peoples. The basic condition for a happy future for our people is, therefore, a final break with all anti-Soviet and anti-Polish tendencies. . . ." [81]

The SED and their political groups were set the task of convincing the German people of the rightness of friendship with the eastern neighbors. A more or less official history of this period claims that great successes were scored by the SED and associated groups.[82] Whatever the true state of Soviet Zone relations with the systems that were to become increasingly integrated with it, it was not until the establishment of the German Democratic Republic in 1949, and its entry into the communist party state system, that integrative processes really began to function.

[81]Walter Ulbricht, "Die Grundlagen der deutsch-polnischen Freundschaft," *Zur Geschichte*, III, 329.
[82]Hans Müller, *Die Entwicklung der SED*, pp. 189-90.

2: THE ENTRY OF THE G.D.R. INTO THE COMMUNIST PARTY STATE SYSTEM

The G.D.R. entered the communist party state system in a period that might be characterized as one of "intensified transition." This was symbolized by the change in status that the Soviet Zone underwent in the fall of 1949; formerly an object of military occupation, it became a state—the German Democratic Republic. However, Red Army troops remained and the political instructions emanated from the Soviet Control Commission in Berlin-Karlshorst rather than from the SMAD. Formal sovereignty was not granted by the Soviet Union until March, 1954. The entry period represented an effort to leave behind the Antifascist Democratic Order and to develop the G.D.R. into one of the People's Democracies. Entry was achieved between the Third Party Congress in July, 1950, and the Second Party Conference in July, 1952.

Demographic Structure

After the entry of the G.D.R. into the communist party state system two religious groups, the Jews and the Jehovah's Witnesses, were singled out for party action.

The Jewish population of the G.D.R. is difficult to determine. In the pre-entry period their numbers must have been small, and it is unlikely that the Jewish community has grown since 1945. A Western source gives the number of Jews in the Soviet Zone and East Berlin in 1946 as 3,100. In 1952 this figure had declined to 2,600 and in 1962, to 1,800.[1] In 1961 there were nine Jewish communities in the G.D.R. located in Schwerin, Magdeburg, Halle, Erfurt, Dresden, Leipzig, Karl-Marx-Stadt, Plauen, and Berlin, which are combined in a *Verband Jüdischer Gemeinden*.[2]

In 1961 an official G.D.R. source declared a result of the equal rights of all religions and races in the G.D.R.: "Many Jewish citizens [work] in responsible positions in both State and Economy as well as in the democratic parties and mass organizations. They take an active part in the fight to preserve peace and to construct a socialistic social order."[3] This has not always been the case. During the SED purge of 1950, Paul Merker was expelled from the party for allegedly having contacts with the "American agent" Noel Field. Two years later Merker was arrested and jailed for being a "subject of the finance-oligarchy of the U.S." At both times Merker was accused of participation in the zionist movement and of fostering Jewish particularism in the G.D.R. Released from jail in 1956, Merker was not politically rehabilitated.[4] A similar fate befell Erich Jungmann

[1]*SBZ von A-Z* (Bonn: Deutscher Bundesverlag, 1963), pp. 221-22; and Wolfram Daniel, "Juden in der Zone," *Sonntagsblatt Staats-Zeitung und Herold* (New York), July 5, 1964.

[2]*Jahrbuch der Deutschen Demokratischen Republik 1961* (East Berlin: Verlag Die Wirtschaft, 1961), p. 94.

[3]*Ibid.*

[4]Carola Stern, *Porträt einer bolschewistischen Partei* (Köln: Verlag für Politik und Wirtschaft, 1957), pp. 119 ff.

who was arrested in 1953 for "zionist deviation." Jung-mann, however, was reinstated in 1956.[5] In this connection it should be noted that the G.D.R. has never made any moves toward restitution for Jewish life and prop-erty lost during the nazi era. Furthermore, East Germany has taken a consistently anti-Israeli position.

Jehovah's Witnesses were subjected to persecution during the nazi era and were in effect eliminated as a group. After the war the activities of the community were renewed and again conflicted with the ruling agents of the state. In 1950 Jehovah's Witnesses were accused of distributing antistate literature and of serving as spies for the imperialists. The sect was declared illegal and several leaders were sentenced to life imprisonment. In all, some 2,175 Jehovah's Witnesses were arrested and jailed.[6]

Belief System

The relative uniformity in the belief system in East Germany during the pre-entry period began to dissolve after 1948. As the pre-entry period ended the emphasis shifted from the basic value of antifascism to the goal of a democratic socialist order. As this shift became more apparent, another shift away from the goals of the Socialist Unity Party was reflected in the change from a mass party to the Party of the New Type and in the addition of SED-controlled parties and mass organizations. The change can be best described as one away from SED leadership toward SED direction.

In official party histories the Third Party Congress of

[5]*SBZ-Biographie* (Bonn and Berlin: Bundesministerium für Gesamtdeutsche Fragen, 1964), p. 166.
[6]*SBZ von A-Z* (1963), pp. 545-46.

the SED in July, 1950, marked the beginning of the second phase of the revolution and the "Dictatorship of the Proletariat." [7] The problem facing the SED at this time consisted of "further raising the fighting power of the working class and also winning over the majority of the people for Socialism, especially the working peasant." [8]

The most important decision of the Third Party Congress, aside from the announcement of the first Five Year Plan, was that the G.D.R. was not yet ready for socialism. Dialectically expressed, there was a contradiction between the economic and political development of the G.D.R. and the development of the "consciousness of the masses that did not allow the question of socialism to be put openly." [9]

In order to develop the consciousness of the masses the SED purged the party membership while stepping up agitation and propaganda. Furthermore, the Two Year Plan of 1949 and 1950 conditioned East Germans to the mechanics of a planned economy. Finally, the G.D.R. became active on the international scene, seeking formal and informal recognition for its place in the international state system.

Social System

Political. With the founding of the G.D.R. in October, 1949, the SED was for all practical purposes estab-

[7]See, for example, Werner Horn, *Die Errichtung der Grundlagen des Sozialismus in der Industrie der DDR (1951-1955)* (East Berlin: Dietz Verlag, 1963), chap. 1.

[8]Werner Horn, *Der Kampf der SED um die Festigung der DDR und den Uebergang zur zweiten Etappe der Revolution (1949-1952)* (East Berlin: Dietz Verlag, 1959), p. 31.

[9]*Ibid.*, p. 81.

lished as *the* state party.[10] Earlier the People's Congress movement, which had begun as an "all-German" organization, became the spearhead of an official mass movement aimed at the transformation of the Soviet Zone into a state. The Third People's Congress of May, 1949, elected a People's Council that later became the provisional People's Legislature of the G.D.R. The SED secured its leadership position in the movement by forcing common lists of candidates on other parties and the mass organizations. In October, 1949, the People's Congress movement became the National Front. Under the influence of the SED members in its leadership, the National Front was the authoritative organization for determining the policies of the parties and mass organizations.

The National Front was the organizational executor of the successful *Gleichschaltung* of the parties and groups that had provided a certain pluralism in the pre-entry period. One communist commentator summed up the situation as follows: "During this time [1949-50] the last great confrontation between the progressive and reactionary elements in the LDPD and CDU took place, with the isolation and exclusion of such representatives of the bourgeoisie within these parties . . . who were in favor of the restoration of capitalism. CDU and LDPD were finally transformed from bourgeois to petit bourgeois parties that recognize the leadership of the working class and its party [the SED]." [11] The ultimate expression of the politics of the

[10]Stern, *Porträt,* pp. 138-41.

[11]Harry Nick, "Zu einigen Grundfragen der zweiten Etappe der volksdemokratischen Revolution in der Deutschen Demokratischen Republik," *Zur Oekonomik der Uebergangsperiode in der Deutschen Demokratischen Republik,* ed. Roland Hauk *et al.* (East Berlin: Dietz Verlag, 1962), pp. 103-4.

entry period was the election of October, 1950. The National Front presented a unified list of candidates for the People's Legislature (*Volkskammer*) during the summer of 1950 which determined that the legislature would have the following representation (more recent figures are given for comparison): [12]

Parties	First legislative period 1949–53 (%)	Fourth legislative period 1963–67 (%)
SED	25.0	25.5
CDU	15.0	10.4
LDPD	15.0	10.4
NDPD	7.5	10.4
DBD	7.5	10.4
FDGB	10.0	13.8
FDJ	5.0	8.1
DK	5.0	4.4
DFD	3.7	6.6
VVN	3.7	–
VDGB	1.3	–
Genossenschaften	1.3	–

As the SED secured its position of influence, it moved to rid itself of all revisionist and potentially revisionist elements in an "audit" or purge of the party membership which had been announced at the Third Party Congress and carried out during the first half of 1951. The purge had three purposes: to form a new party cadre; to eliminate undesirable members; and to generate enthusiasm for party activities.

The party audit was conducted by establishing examination committees (6,000 with a total of 30,000 members) that received the credentials from all SED

[12]Horn, *Der Kampf,* pp. 66-67; and *Statistisches Jahrbuch der DDR 1966,* p. 581.

members and candidates. Each individual was interviewed to determine his suitability. In essence the entire party membership "resigned" and was reinstated, struck from the rolls, excluded from the party, or set back from full to candidate membership. From the examining committees, which had been made up of the most reliable elements, the party hoped to recruit new leadership with "deep insight" into the functioning of the party apparatus.[13]

Prior to the purge the SED had a total membership (including candidates) of 1,316,700.[14] Official figures show that 150,696 members and candidates were either expelled from the party or struck from the membership rolls. However, careful recalculation of these figures by Joachim Schultz has shown that the real figure was 68,493.[15] Furthermore, this refiguring indicates that the party was not as amenable to becoming the New Type as the SED leadership might have hoped. The number of individuals who did not submit to the audit was 31,700, or within the limits of probable error for the figure given of those expelled from the party (31,451). It is likely that the vast majority of those actually expelled were those who would not play the game. This was a particularly embarrassing situation for the party leadership since most of those who would not go along were workers. Furthermore, complete party organizations in some large People's Enterprises refused to turn in their party books and cards, thus indicating a substantial degree of opposition.[16]

[13]For a general account see: Stern, *Porträt,* pp. 130-35.

[14]Joachim Schultz, *Der Funktionär in der Einheitspartei* (Stuttgart and Düsseldorf: Ring Verlag, 1956), p. 135.

[15]*Ibid.,* p. 137; and Horn, *Der Kampf,* pp. 88-89.

[16]Schultz, *Der Funtionär,* pp. 137-38.

The third purpose of the purge—to generate enthusiasm for party activities—involved a series of self-commitments that members and candidates undertook or were supposed to undertake. These self-commitments included pledges to introduce new work methods—largely imported from the Soviet Union—and participation in special party courses in ideology. Only one-third of the membership undertook self-commitments and these individuals were mainly white collar workers who saw in self-commitment a means for maintaining or strengthening their positions in the bureaucracy. Relatively few workers participated.[17]

In all the purge was mild. The party leadership had wanted to test the condition of the party. They discovered in the many interviews and discussions accompanying the purge that a Party of the New Type had not been achieved. The problem of opportunism among party members and functionaries was fully revealed to the leadership. This problem has continued to plague the SED. The actions that could be taken against individuals not in sympathy with the SED and its leadership were limited by the economic importance of certain groups—such as skilled workers and intellectuals—which could avail themselves of the open border in Berlin.

Economic. During the entry period the transition to the planned economy was aided by the Two Year Plan of 1949-50. Actually this had been preceded by a "half-

---

[17]*Ibid.*, pp. 141-42. See also: Walter Ulbricht, "Die Verbesserung der Arbeit der Parteileitungen in Verbindung mit der Ueberprüfung der Mitglieder und Kandidaten," *Zur Geschichte der Deutschen Arbeiterbewegung* (East Berlin: Dietz Verlag, 1960), IV, 141-43.

year plan." However, the real effort was directed toward fulfillment of the Two Year Plan announced in June, 1948.[18] The purpose of the Two Year Plan was pedagogical in the broadest sense. According to Walter Ulbricht, "the [degree] of conviction of the workers, salaried employees, engineers and working people is even more important than the best [plan] figures that we have worked out!" [19]

By lowering production costs and raising worker productivity, the economy of the G.D.R. was to be made self-sufficient in spite of the East-West split. A German *Stachanov* was found in Adolf Hennecke and an "agitprop" movement was invented to spur on the workers. Incentive wages were introduced along with a host of other gimmicks. The goal of the plan was to reach 81 per cent of 1936 production. A modest goal, in keeping with the purpose of generating enthusiasm through participation and fulfillment,[20] it was reached in one and one-half years, in time for the Third Party Congress.[21] By the end of the two years, 1936 production levels had been achieved,[22] and the basis for the First Five Year Plan (1951-55) had been laid.

Degree of integration of G.D.R. with other systems.
The degree of integration of the G.D.R. with other

[18]Walter Ulbricht, "Der Zweijahrplan zur Wiederherstellung und Entwicklung der Friedenswirtschaft," *Zur sozialistischen Entwicklung der Volkswirtschaft seit 1945* (East Berlin: Dietz Verlag, 1959), pp. 111-38. See also: "Der deutsche Zweijahrplan," *Ibid.*, pp. 139-49.

[19]*Ibid.*, p. 142.

[20]*Ibid.*, p. 137.

[21]Walter Ulbricht, "Der Fünfjahrplan und die Perspektiven der Volkswirtschaft," *Zur Geschichte,* III, 649.

[22]Wolfgang Stolper, *The Structure of the East German Economy* (Cambridge, Mass.: Harvard University Press, 1960), p. 251.

systems has a "positive-negative" element; that is, the degree of identification that the G.D.R. exhibited in any one period was, at least in part, a function of its separation from the West. The propaganda effort during the entry period was directed, in spite of its basic contradiction, toward an image of a unified Germany that denied the social and economic system of the Federal Republic of Germany. Indeed, one of the basic problems the G.D.R. had to cope with was the presence of an outrageously successful capitalist system "next door" which shared its own common cultural heritage. The constant comparison that the G.D.R. citizen made to measure his own state of well-being was not with a communist utopia, but rather with the capitalist presence of the Federal Republic that, until August 13, 1961, was accessible through Berlin. On the "positive" side the need to identify with the Soviet Union and the People's Democracies was stressed above all because the truncated economy of the G.D.R. could find there an area into which it could be integrated. (Table 8 shows the early development of G.D.R. foreign trade.)

Although interzonal trade increased during this period, it did not achieve the internal exchange levels that existed between the same areas of prewar Germany. It must be noted, however, that the expansion and construction of G.D.R. industries were intended to provide compensation for the goods cut off by the zonal boundary. This had the effect of moving the G.D.R. economy toward independence rather than toward the integration that might have been expected and that would have obviated the development of heavy industry—the priority in the economic plans.[23]

[23]*Ibid.*, p. 11.

With its establishment in 1949, new possibilities for the G.D.R. were offered in the area of international relations. Official statements emphasized that relations between the G.D.R. and other states would be on the basis of "full equality." In the 1949-52 period the G.D.R. was party to a total of 137 treaties.[24] The great majority of these were with the Soviet Union and the People's Democracies.

[24]Lothar Kapsa, *Zusammenstellung der von der "Deutschen Demokratischen Republik" seit deren Gründung (7. 10. 1949) abgeschlossenen internationalen Verträge und Vereinbarungen,* 3rd ed. (Bonn: Archiv für Gesamtdeutsche Fragen, 1962).

3: THE INTENSIVE SOCIALIST DEVELOPMENT OF THE G.D.R.

The period of intensive socialist development began with the first Five Year Plan in 1951 and was re-emphasized at the Second Party Conference of the SED in July, 1952. There Walter Ulbricht declared that:

The democratic and economic development as well as the consciousness of the working class and the majority of the employed are now developed to the point that the construction of socialism has become the basic mission. . . .

In concurrence with the suggestions coming from the working class, from the working peasants and other circles of the employed, the Central Committee of the Socialist Unity Party has resolved to suggest to the Second Party Conference that socialism be constructed according to plan in the German Democratic Republic.[1]

By the summer of 1952 the G.D.R. had achieved the status of a People's Democracy; production was increasing; international contacts were being made; two purges had been conducted within the SED; and SED

[1]Walter Ulbricht, "Die Gegenwärtige Lage und die neuen Aufgaben der Sozialistischen Einheitspartei Deutschlands," *Zur Geschichte der Deutschen Arbeiterbewegung* (East Berlin: Dietz Verlag, 1960), IV, 407.

influence had penetrated and permeated all parties and mass organizations. It appeared as if the first phase of intensive, Stalinist development—which went under the slogan of building the foundations of socialism in the G.D.R.—could proceed according to plan.

Belief System

Basic values and goals.   The distribution of basic values and goals in this period, as illustrated by the uprising of June 16 and 17, 1953, indicated that all was not well. The first Five Year Plan could not rely on much help from either the Soviet Union or the other People's Democracies, so emphasis had to be placed on increases in worker productivity and improvements in the utilization of raw materials if the plan goals were to be realized. The latter emphasis put pressure on the managers of the People's Enterprises (*Volkseigene Betriebe*—VEB),[2] whereas the former demanded great sacrifices from the working class.

Workers' productivity was raised by increasing production norms. Norm increases were accelerated in 1952 and 1953 at a rate that went beyond what the workers would tolerate. Increased norms were accompanied by massive "agitprop" campaigns managed by the SED and the Free German Labor Union Federation (FDGB), which had become an instrument for carrying out party directions. Individuals and brigades of workers pledged themselves to meet plan goals before scheduled dates. Such carefully staged actions were held up as models for others to follow and became the bases for still higher norms in a pattern familiar in the

[2]K. Valentin Müller, *Die Manager in der Sowjetzone* (Köln and Opladen: Westdeutscher Verlag, 1962).

Soviet Union. However, the intensity of the drive was greater than in other East European states.

An inexact but indicative measure of internal dissatisfaction and reaction to the Stalinist system at this time was the emigration from the G.D.R. In 1951 the movement ranged from 11,583 to 17,389 people per month. In 1952 the low was 7,227 in January; a high of 23,331 was reached in September. The monthly average for the first six months of 1953 was in excess of 37,000 people, with a low of 22,396 and a high of 58,605.[3]

The SED was not blind to these developments, but its leadership was unsure about what measures should be undertaken to ease the situation. To institute significant reforms would be to admit errors that would, in effect, question the soundness of the leadership and its policies. Were the SED not to alter its course, a disaster that would echo throughout the Communist Bloc might well result.

After Stalin's death Malenkov and the new Soviet leadership shifted emphasis away from heavy industry and toward consumer goods. This gave the SED leadership an opportunity to relax the drive toward heavy industrialization and agricultural collectivization and to ease the campaign against churches and private businesses. In spite of this opportunity the SED alone could not produce a satisfactory reform program. Ulbricht and the lower party organization were not as flexible as the higher functionaries: Ulbricht was devoted to the Stalinist order; and the local party leadership had no

[3]"The Trend of Refugees from the Soviet Zone and the Soviet Sector of Berlin," Table compiled by the Federal Ministry for Expellees, Refugees, and War Victims (Bonn, 1962). These figures include only those individuals applying for emergency reception in the Federal Republic.

desire to abandon the hard line, since relaxation might threaten their party careers.

The SED finally did proclaim a New Course.[4] The new Soviet leadership had repeatedly urged the SED to review its situation.[5] But the SED was not moved until June 5, when Vladimir Semjonow returned to Berlin as chief of the Soviet Control Commission. Semjonow brought with him the text of the main points that the SED Politburo finally adopted.[6] The New Course admitted previous failures and mistakes and generally promised a more relaxed tempo in the socialization process. However, spiraling work norms were not affected by the New Course. When new norms were defended on June 16, strike action began among construction workers in the ideologically vital Stalinallee of East Berlin.[7] As the uprising spread, demands escalated from norms revision to free elections and an end to the Ulbricht regime.

Two aspects of the revolt are of particular interest: the first is the leaderless character of the uprising; the second is the reaction of the SED leadership. There appears to be no evidence to support the notion that the June revolt in the G.D.R. had any central leadership from either within or without. The official East

[4]*SBZ von A-Z* (1963), p. 228.

[5]Carola Stern, *Porträt einer bolschewistischen Partei* (Köln: Verlag für Politik und Wirtschaft, 1957), pp. 154-55.

[6]Arnulf Baring, *Der 17. Juni 1953* (Köln and Berlin: Kiepenheuer und Witsch, 1965), pp. 41-42.

[7]Many accounts are available in addition to Baring's. See, for example: Stefan Brant, *Der Aufstand—Vorgeschichte, Geschichte und Deutung des 17. Juni 1953* (Stuttgart: Steingrüben Verlag, 1954). [Available also in English as: *The East German Rising 17th June 1953* (London: Thames and Hudson, 1955).] See also: Rainer Hildebrandt, *The Explosion: The Uprising Behind the Iron Curtain* (New York: Duell, Sloan and Pearce, 1955).

German versions of the events speak of fascist provocation and the role of U.S. imperialism.[8] Yet no organizations, circles, or personalities have been associated with the revolt. Furthermore, the conduct of the crowds and their unco-ordinated action indicates a lack of focus that leadership should provide. Finally, an eyewitness report indicates that even relatively homogeneous mobs refused to select either individuals or delegations to negotiate with those party officials brave enough to face the masses.[9]

The reaction of the party leadership ranged from absolute loyalty, through incredulity, to participation in the revolt. Soon after the Soviet troops had restored order, the SED issued an official version of the events and assessed how successful efforts had been at securing a Party of the New Type. Aside from a small minority of functionaries who were prepared to meet any situation with their party convictions, the SED rank and file proved to be unreliable security for the leadership against all eventualities. The great number of party members who sought the protection of Soviet power, who hid or otherwise distanced themselves from the party in its hour of need, were too many for comfort. Suddenly Walter Ulbricht redesignated the SED a mass party.[10] And the standard placebo, better ideological training, was prescribed.

Among the SED leadership a tactical opposition to Ulbricht gained momentum with the rising dissatisfac-

[8]Werner Horn, *Die Errichtung der Grundlagen des Sozialismus in der Industrie der DDR (1951-1955)* (East Berlin: Dietz Verlag, 1963), pp. 208-22.

[9]Fritz Schenk, "Wie die Regierung den 17. Juni erlebte," *SBZ-Archiv,* XII, no. 10 (May, 1962), 150.

[10]Walter Ulbricht, "Die gegenwärtige Lage und der neue Kurs der Partei," *Zur Geschichte,* IV, 622.

tion in the spring of 1953. Wilhelm Zaisser, Minister for State Security, and Rudolf Herrnstadt, the editor of the official party newspaper, *Neues Deutschland,* constructed a platform directed against the leadership of Walter Ulbricht and circulated it among those functionaries whom they thought would support their position. Thus Ulbricht was faced with a two-fold threat during the events of June 17. In dealing with the revolt itself, he ultimately had the support of Soviet troops. In coming to terms with the party opposition, he had to rely on his own considerable skill at party infighting. His skill was more than adequate to meet the challenge: Zaisser was identified with Beria, and Herrnstadt was accused of equivocation during the crisis. Both were degraded to ordinary party membership status.[11]

Finally, a discussion of the distribution of beliefs and values relating to the 1953 revolt must take into account Arnulf Baring's findings on internal support for the uprising.[12] The strikes and demonstrations were, by and large, products of the working class. The middle classes were unsure—the revolt had come suddenly and its direction was uncertain. Under the circumstances the safest course was to do nothing. The intelligentsia, particularly the technicians and engineers, had been bought off with privileges, special treatment, and high salaries. Their posture was one of cool loyalty to the government on June 17.[13] The revolt, then, was not a mass uprising on a broad scale. Moreover, the Soviets did not grind the revolt beneath the treads of their tanks. The momentum of June 16 and 17 had been lost by the time the Soviet army made its move. (For

[11]Stern, *Porträt,* pp. 163-69.
[12]Baring, *Der 17. Juni 1953,* pp. 83-85.
[13]*Ibid.,* p. 84.

those accustomed to thinking of the revolt in terms of pictures showing East Germans throwing rocks—not Molotov cocktails—at Soviet tanks, this may come as something of a shock.)

The leaderless and divided opposition among the people and the party opposition without a mass base that characterized the June, 1953, revolt are typical of opposition in East Germany. Neither the Herrnstadt-Zaisser coalition and its successors, nor the workers, had a realistic chance against Walter Ulbricht and the Soviet presence. This configuration holds for the basic values and goals and for their propagation in the G.D.R. The values of the elite add up to what might be termed support for a Soviet Germany. The assimilation of these values by the masses was uneven and will remain so as long as there are religious institutions, right and left dissenters, and remnants of the bourgeoisie. However, there is no solid basis uniting dissenters in an effective opposition.

Social System

Economic. The New Course that grew out of the increased intensity of socialist development in 1952 and the first six months of 1953 was, for all intents and purposes, an interlude. Many concessions made by the SED were rescinded within a year after the revolt; by the summer of 1955 Walter Ulbricht had proclaimed the end of the New Course at the twenty-fourth meeting of the SED Central Committee.[14] The end of the New

[14]Walter Ulbricht, "Die Warschauer Konferenz und die neuen Aufgaben in Deutschland," *Zur sozialistischen Entwicklung der Volkswirtschaft seit 1945* (East Berlin: Dietz Verlag, 1959), pp. 474-77.

Course did not mean a return to the pre-June, 1953, policies in all their harshness; but Ulbricht made it clear that some interpretations of the New Course had made of it a Wrong Course and that the Party had never intended to stray from one of its basic objectives —the development of heavy industry.

The development of heavy industry was intended to act as a base for other G.D.R. industries. The drive toward a balanced or more independent economic system continued under the rubric of "undoing the damage done by war." The first Five Year Plan had as its goal the doubling of 1936 production levels by the end of 1955.[15] It is extremely difficult to tell if the aim was fulfilled, in part because 1936 and 1955 production levels are extremely difficult to compare.[16] It is clear from the official appraisal of the first Five Year Plan and other figures that the G.D.R. economy had made considerable progress toward strengthening its weaker sectors, even though heavy industry, hindered by the New Course detour, fell short of the plan goal by 22.9 per cent.[17] At the same time the G.D.R. economy was able to expand its exports, indicating its future importance as a partner in the Socialist Bloc.

The East German economic situation was further improved when reparations payments to the Soviet Union were formally ended in 1953. A formal stopping of reparations did not immediately halt Soviet exploitation. Heinz Köhler suggests that for at least the

[15]*Ibid.,* p. 273.

[16]Wolfgang Stolper, *The Structure of the East German Economy* (Cambridge, Mass.: Harvard University Press, 1960), pp. 65-66.

[17]Walter Ulbricht, "Der zweite Fünfjahrplan und der Aufbau des Sozialismus in der Deutschen Demokratischen Republik," *Zur sozialistischen Entwicklung,* pp. 517-37.

1954-56 period the Soviet Union "shifted exploitation to the commercial realm." [18] The question of Soviet advantage or preference in trade with the G.D.R. has occurred again and again to the present.

Internally the publicly owned sector of the economy continued to grow (see Table 9). Most of this growth came from the private sector with a minor increase in the joint corporations with state participation.

Military. According to the Potsdam Agreements, Germany was to be permanently demilitarized. However, it was not long before quasi-military organizations began to appear in the Soviet Zone of Germany. In 1946 a centralized People's Police was established, followed a short while later by a Border Police force of nearly 10,000 men. In the years 1948-51 the police units expanded to a military establishment of about 65,000. In 1952 the various police forces were reorganized and a part of them placed in barracks units. These units were the first army of the G.D.R. Training followed Red Army procedures and the first uniform adopted was similar to the Red Army uniform and carried the same rank designations. The training and political indoctrination of the barracks police units were supervised by "Sovietniks,"—Soviet army officers who served as military advisers.

At the Second Party Conference of the SED in July, 1952, Walter Ulbricht spoke on the "Meaning and Character of the People's Army." [19] In the course of his remarks Ulbricht developed the notion of just and

---

[18]Heinz Köhler, *Economic Integration in the Soviet Bloc* (New York: Frederick A. Praeger, 1965), p. 358.

[19]Ulbricht, "Die gegenwärtige Lage," *Zur Geschichte,* pp. 422-24.

unjust war, and the need of the patriotic citizen of the
G.D.R. to support the military establishment necessitated by the machinations of the Imperialists. The new
military forces of the G.D.R. were to be filled with
hatred for the Imperialists and with brotherhood for
the Soviet Union and the People's Democracies.

In the same year, 1952, two paramilitary organizations were created to broaden the support for the military: the industrial combat groups and the Society for
Sport and Technology. The Society for Sport and Technology has as its objective the premilitary training for
fourteen- to twenty-four-year-old males. In 1962 the
society had about 450,000 members.[20] The industrial
and combat groups have as their mission the military
training of adults between the ages of twenty-five and
sixty. The combat groups are organized in industrial
units and agrarian collectives. As in the case of the
Society for Sport and Technology, membership in the
combat groups is theoretically voluntary, but in fact
forced—usually by directed peer-group pressure. In
1963 the number of men in combat groups was esti-
mated at 320,000, of whom some 150,000 were considered combat ready.[21]

In the spring of 1955 a campaign for volunteers for
the barracks units of the People's Police received new
impetus under the direction of Willi Stoph, who later
became the first G.D.R. Defense Minister.[22] The campaign was directed toward the Warsaw Conference in

[20]*SBZ von A-Z* (1963), p. 450.

[21]Fritz Kopp, "Streitkräfte und Milizen," *SBZ-Archiv,* XIII,
no. 14 (July, 1962), 217.

[22]*SBZ-Biographie* (Bonn and Berlin: Bundesministerium für
Gesamtdeutsche Fragen, 1964), pp. 343-44. Stoph is now Deputy
Chairman of the Council of State.

May, 1955, at which the G.D.R. hoped to become an openly remilitarized partner of the Soviet Union and the People's Democracies. The hopes of the G.D.R. leadership were not immediately realized because the Polish and Czech delegations to the conference were strongly opposed to a new German army. Minimally, Poland and Czechoslovakia demanded a series of treaties guaranteeing the border arrangements between them and the G.D.R. before agreeing to rearmament. It was not until January, 1956, that Polish and Czech objections were overcome, permitting the renaming of G.D.R. units as the National People's Army and the establishment of a Ministry for National Defense; [23] the addition of armored sea and air units followed quickly.

Symbolically, the uniform of the National People's Army was no longer patterned on the Soviet model, but returned, apparently on Soviet suggestion, to the grey Wehrmacht uniform, retaining the Soviet steel helmet. This combination presents an ambiguous and not entirely happy image as honor guards pass before East European visitors using the parade march goose step.

Degree of Integration of the G.D.R. with Other Systems

The economic sector of the G.D.R. system continued to be the major area of integrative activity in the 1952-56 period. In spite of the apparent paradox, the move toward increased economic independence by the development of heavy industries and better utilization of those raw materials available with East Germany made the G.D.R. a stronger and therefore more easily

[23]Stern, *Porträt,* pp. 174-75.

integrated partner within the system of the Council for Mutual Economic Assistance (COMECON). Such an economy could contribute better to the other East European economies and complement that of the Soviet Union. The formal end of reparations in this period can be taken as an indication of the Soviet desire to strengthen the East German economy.

In foreign trade the G.D.R. moved from an "unfavorable balance" at the outset of the first Five Year Plan to an export surplus in 1955. The share of the Socialist Bloc in this trade was steadily above 70 per cent, whereas the absolute amount of trade nearly trebled in the period between 1950 and 1955.[24]

During the preparatory stages of the second Five Year Plan, activity in COMECON was on the rise with Council meetings in March and June, 1954, and December, 1955. The activity was directed toward an attempted co-ordination of plan production among participants and the establishment of permanent committees to oversee production in various industrial sectors.[25] The combination of a relatively stronger G.D.R. economy within a developing integrative institution (COMECON) provided the G.D.R. with the opportunity of sharing in bloc decision-making processes. The transition was symbolized by the granting of sovereignty to the G.D.R. by the Soviet Union on March 25, 1954.[26]

[24]*SBZ von A-Z* (1963), p. 51.

[25]Konstantin Pritzel, *Die wirtschaftliche Integration der sowjetischen Besatzungszone Deutschlands in den Ostblock und ihre politische Aspekte* (Bonn and Berlin: Bundesministerium für Gesamtdeutsche Fragen, 1962), pp. 58-59.

[26]*Geschichtliche Zeittafel der Deutschen Demokratischen Republik* (East Berlin: Kongress-Verlag, 1959), p. 155.

4: THE THAW: 1956-60

The thaw period in the G.D.R. had its origins somewhat before the Twentieth Party Congress of the Communist Party of the Soviet Union (CPSU). Since June, 1953, ideas of revolt had been circulating which could be characterized as revisionist. But it was not until after the attack on Stalin became known that these ideas began circulating actively, even openly. The revisionist ideas of the thaw can best be examined in terms of the belief system of the G.D.R. in the post-1956 period.

Belief System

Basic values and goals. The promulgators of the official G.D.R. value system after 1945 were the members of the SED and the leaders of the mass organizations. The disparity between official values and working-class values had come to light in the first major revolt within the communist system during the summer of 1953. It had been a revolt of the workers, leaderless and without direction.

Three years later another revolt was underway in the G.D.R. This time it was a revolt of party and nonparty intellectuals, who were acting on their interpretations of Marxism-Leninism and the examples of Hungary and Poland. In 1956 the revolt had a spokesman in Wolfgang Harich, who proclaimed a "platform" for the reformation of the SED and the G.D.R. on Marxist-Leninist grounds and principles. In contrast to the events in Hungary and Poland, the intellectual leadership that planned to reform post-Stalin communism in order to serve the communist ideal neither sought nor sparked mass support.

Harich's platform,[1] which had as its goal the elimination of Stalinism and dogmatism, included such elements as a parliamentary road to socialism, the dissolving of the Secret State Security Service, and the establishment of Workers' Councils in the People's Enterprises.[2] Along with Harich's political program were found the revisionist arguments of historians (Jürgen Kuczynski and Joachim Streisand), agrarian economists (such as Kurt Vieweg), and economists (Fritz Behrens and Arne Benary) to name a few.[3] In the pages of the literary weekly, *Sonntag,* and among editors of the *Aufbau-Verlag,* as well as in certain institutes of the German Academy of Sciences in Berlin and the Universities of Berlin and Leipzig, discussions touching every aspect of life in the G.D.R. were underway in the late spring and summer of 1956.

Throughout these months Harich was in contact with the Social Democratic Party of the Federal Re-

[1]Fritz Raddatz, "The Case of Wolfgang Harich," *Encounter,* XXIV, no. 2 (February, 1965), 91-92.

[2]Karl Wilhelm Fricke, *Selbstbehauptung und Wiederstand in der Sowjetischen Besatzungszone Deutschlands* (Bonn and Berlin: Deutscher Bundesverlag, 1964), p. 131.

[3]P. C. Ludz, "Revisionistische Konzeptionen von 1956/57 in der 'DDR'," *Moderne Welt,* II, no. 4 (1960/61), 353 ff.

public, with the Petofi Circle in Hungary (through the good offices of Georg Lukacs), and with the Soviet Embassy in Berlin. Harich delivered his platform to the Soviet Embassy after he could find no one willing to present it to the SED leadership. He was determined to proceed by legal means and to avoid any possibility of an uprising.

As in 1953, Walter Ulbricht was able to move effectively to neutralize the opposition. Harich and his followers were arrested shortly after the Polish and Hungarian events had passed their climax. In trials conducted in the spring and summer of 1957, Harich and his followers were given sentences of from two to ten years in prison even though, strictly speaking, they had done nothing illegal.[4]

The fate of other revisionists was less harsh. Behrens and Benary managed to avoid punishment by publishing abject declarations of self-criticism.[5] Professor Ernst Bloch, the intellectual father of the Harich group in Germany, was forced to retire from his chair of philosophy at the Karl Marx University in Leipzig.

The net effect of revisionist activity in the thaw period has been summed up as "revisionism without revision," though it should not be taken as the end of revisionist thought and tendencies in the G.D.R.[6] The party has constantly had to fight to maintain its line.

[4]Heinz Zöger, "Die politischen Hintergründe der Harich-Prozesse," *SBZ-Archiv*, XI, no. 13 (July, 1960), 199. As a result of an amnesty granted on the fifteenth anniversary of the G.D.R. Harich was released from prison.

[5]"Erklärung des Genossen Prof. Dr. Fritz Behrens. Erklärung des Genossen Arne Benary," *Neuer Weg*, XV, no. 9 (1960), 650-52.

[6]Ludz, "Revisionistische Konzeptionen," p. 365.

This is particularly true of the intellectuals, whose views of communism and Marxism differ from Ulbricht's.[7]

In attempting to close the gap between the SED leadership and views of various groups in society, two broad countermeasures were introduced under the rubrics "socialist morality" and the "socialist school."

Socialist morality has its origins in Leninist thought and generally means that whatever fosters socialism is moral. At the Fifth Party Congress in July, 1958, Walter Ulbricht proclaimed the "Ten Socialist Commandments" that were to become the basis for a new emphasis on the inculcation of socialist morality in the G.D.R.[8] With atheistic parallels to religious ceremonies —such as the "socialist" baptism, confirmation, and wedding, which were either introduced or strongly re-emphasized in 1957 and after—the SED tried to develop a new type of socialist being who would presumably be more easily integrated into an international socialist community.

As the second countermeasure of 1958, the transition to the socialist school was announced as the goal of educators in the G.D.R.[9] The time was ripe for a change because by 1958 children reaching school age had been born after the establishment of the G.D.R. Coincidental with educational reforms, Walter Ulbricht called for an evaluation of Soviet experience in developing new methods of education.

To educate socialist citizens it was thought necessary

[7]See: Martin Jänicke, *Der dritte Weg* (Köln: Neuer Deutscher Verlag, 1964); and P. C. Ludz's review of Jänicke, "Ein Mythos vom dritten Weg," *SBZ-Archiv*, XVI, no. 8 (April, 1965), 119-23.

[8]*Protokoll des V. Parteitages der Sozialistischen Einheitspartei Deutschlands* (East Berlin: Dietz Verlag, 1959), I, 160-61.

[9]*Ibid.*, pp. 164-73.

to bring the pupil closer to the productive processes in order that he might learn at a very early age to love work and to accustom himself to physical labor. Late in 1959 a law was passed providing for a uniform ten-class, general education, polytechnical school.[10] A twelve-class or extended high school was maintained to provide for those students going directly into the universities. Theory and practice were to be combined in both systems in such a way that pupils would actually participate in the productive process once a week ("day in production"). The goal of this sort of education, apart from the hoped-for psychological tie to work, was the qualification of students for a trade. Furthermore, the pupils provided a source of low-cost labor during their practical experience.[11]

According to the law cited above, the education of the socialist citizen was to begin at the age of three. Kindergartens were to prepare children for socialist life, with special attention given to the children of employed mothers.[12] The new order in education was clearly aimed at intensifying the use of labor resources.

Social System

Political. The political system of the G.D.R., which had been structurally quite stable at least since the

[10]"Gesetz über die sozialistische Entwicklung des Schulwesens in der Deutschen Demokratischen Republik vom 2. Dezember 1959," *Dokumentation zu Fragen des Erziehungs- und Bildungswesens in der "DDR"* (Berlin: Verband Deutscher Studentenschaften, n.d.), pp. 6-13.

[11]The presence of pupils and students has not always contributed to the efficiency of production operations. Interview with an electrical engineer, formerly of the G.D.R., at the Notaufnahmelager Marienfelde. Berlin, March, 1962.

[12]"Gesetz über die sozialistische Entwicklung," p. 13.

1954 Party Statute, was materially altered in September, 1960, with the creation of the Council of State. The Council of State, the only chairman of which has been Walter Ulbricht, is unique in the communist state system, the closest thing to it being the Presidium of the Supreme Soviet. However, in contrast to the Soviet Presidium, the Council of State is not an arm of the legislature and is not made up of Union Republic representatives. Furthermore, the Council of State can issue decrees with the force of law.[13] In essence, the creation of the Council of State with Ulbricht at its head meant that the personality cult was to continue in the G.D.R. in spite of the Twentieth Party Congress of the Communist Party of the Soviet Union. Ulbricht was, as Chairman of the Council of State, head of state, head of party, and with the advancing age of Minister-president Otto Grotewohl, head of government as well. A few months before the establishment of the Council of State, Ulbricht had stressed the idea that little had to be done to accommodate the Soviet line of collective leadership because the SED Central Committee had always met regularly.[14] In fact Ulbricht's control, especially after the elimination of the Schirdewan-Wollweber opposition in early 1958, was secure at all important levels of political activity in the G.D.R.

Economic. The two economic plans—the second Five Year Plan (1956-60) and the Seven Year Plan (1959-65) —had major integrative implications for the G.D.R. The second Five Year Plan was to concentrate on heavy industry and to bring about an increase in productivity

[13]Carola Stern, "Der Staatsrat der 'DDR,' " *SBZ-Archiv,* XI, no. 18 (September, 1960), 274.

[14]Victor Kagel, "Neuer Stil—altes Dogma," *SBZ-Archiv,* XI, no. 10 (May, 1960), 152.

of 155 per cent over 1955, with a 150 per cent increase in individual worker productivity. According to Walter Ulbricht, "the Second Five Year Plan can be distinguished from the First Five Year Plan in that it has been coordinated with the Plans of all Socialist States." In the same speech Ulbricht outlined the rapidly increasing importance of East German industrial might in the bloc.[15] Aside from the concentration on heavy industry, the second Five Year Plan united the G.D.R. and other bloc states in emphasizing quality of production with a view to an intensive export campaign.

The economic consequences of bloc unrest in 1956 seriously disrupted the second Five Year Plan. Following the lead of the Soviet Union, which had broken off its sixth Five Year Plan in September, 1957, the G.D.R. shifted to a Seven Year Plan for the period 1959-65.[16] At the Fifth Party Congress of the SED Walter Ulbricht still spoke of the second and third Five Year Plans, but in terms of developments in the next seven years. The main economic goal of these seven years for the U.S.S.R. was to surpass the U.S. in agricultural production. Not to be outdone, the G.D.R. selected the Federal Republic of Germany as its competitor and vowed to match and surpass per capita consumption in foodstuffs and consumer goods by 1961. Understating the case, Ulbricht said, "The Main Economic Objective has a deep political content..." [17]

[15]Walter Ulbricht, "Der zweite Fünfjahrplan und der Aufbau des Sozialismus in der Deutschen Demokratischen Republik," *Zur sozialistischen Entwicklung der Volkswirtschaft seit 1945* (East Berlin: Dietz Verlag, 1959), pp. 540-43.

[16]Konstantin Pritzel, *Die wirtschaftliche Integration der sowjetischen Besatzungszone Deutschlands in den Ostblock und ihre politische Aspekte* (Bonn and Berlin: Bundesministerium für Gesamtdeutsche Fragen, 1962), p. 112.

[17]*Protokoll des V. Parteitages*, I, 69.

In spite of long-term, bilateral trade agreements with the Soviet Union and other People's Democracies, the Seven Year Plan failed.[18] One reason for its failure was the harsh enforcement of the mass collectivization of agriculture in the spring of 1960.[19] In 1959 the Agrarian Collectives (LPG) accounted for 43.5 per cent of the area under cultivation in East Germany, whereas in 1960 this figure rose to 85.0 per cent. In terms of acreage the shift between 1959 and 1960 was from 2,794,306 hectares to 5,384,365.[20] (See Table 10 for details about the development of collectivization.) The abruptness of the change caused economic dislocations throughout the entire G.D.R. economy and put the goal of matching the Federal Republic in per capita food consumption out of reach, which in turn necessitated basic changes in other plan goals.

G.D.R. as a Self-Fulfilling Unit

During the period of the thaw the economic dependence of the G.D.R. on the partner states of COMECON increased, especially since the partner states supplied raw materials, notably coal and oil. To the extent that it turned away from the move toward autarchy, the G.D.R. became less able to fulfill its own goals without dependence on others in the communist system. As a result it attempted to move closer to the other more developed states in the system.

[18]Pritzel, *Die wirtschaftliche Integration,* p. 112 and Fritz Schenk, "Der Siebenjahrplan und seine Vorgänger," *SBZ-Archiv,* XI, no. 14 (July, 1960), 214-17.

[19]Siegfried Göllner, "Das Bauernlegen in Mitteldeutschland," *SBZ-Archiv,* XI, no. 7 (April, 1960), 97-101.

[20]*Handbuch der Deutschen Demokratischen Republik* (East Berlin: Staatsverlag, n.d.), p. 403.

In November, 1959, a Czech delegation paid a visit to the G.D.R. Relations between the G.D.R. and Czechoslovakia were not founded on the basis of spontaneous mutual love and trust. Nonetheless, they were part of a larger state system, and it was to their advantage to find a means of mutually advantageous participation in the system. A partial solution was found in directing anti-German sentiment toward the Federal Republic of Germany while seeking long-term economic arrangements between Czechoslovakia and the G.D.R.[21]

East Germany and Czechoslovakia are the most economically sophisticated European allies of the U.S.S.R. and they form a vital triangle. Randal Cruikshanks has illustrated the importance of the East Berlin-Prague-Moscow triad in a correlation matrix of the 747 bilateral treaties between the G.D.R. and the communist party states (1949-62).[22] (See Table 11 for the raw data; the correlation matrix will be found in Table 12.) The highest correlation to be found in the system is between the diad G.D.R.–Soviet Union and G.D.R.–Czechoslovakia at .706.

Compatibility of Demands Relevant to Integration

Formulated by the elite of the G.D.R. During the thaw the leading position of the U.S.S.R. was challenged in the political platform formulated by Wolf-

[21]"Die Achse Moskau-Pankow-Prag," *SBZ-Archiv,* X, no. 23 (December, 1959), 353-54.

[22]Randal L. Cruikshanks, "A Technique for Measuring Stability and Change in the East German Political System" (Paper read at the 1966 meeting of the Pacific Northwest Political Science Association, Salem, Oregon).

gang Harich. Even though Harich recognized the Soviet Union as the "first and strongest socialist state of the World," he felt that the combination of the backwardness of old Russia, the lack of a democratic tradition, and the schematic transfer of de-Stalinization to the People's Democracies had brought the leadership pretensions of the U.S.S.R. to an end.[23] Though not always as sharply stated as in Harich's platform, other revisionists of the "national" school, insofar as they sought a "German" or "third" road to socialism, dissented from the integration pattern imposed by the Soviet-supported elite, hoping, in part, to preserve the chances for German reunification.

However, Walter Ulbricht never seriously deviated from the sovietization-integration line. Since he and like-minded functionaries were in control of the SED and the mass organizations, the general political line was kept on the same course. The contents of educational materials and the activities of all organizations are aimed at creating a bond of friendship with other socialist states. How successful this was in terms of influencing the attitudes of the G.D.R. population is an open question in the absence of contemporary empirical studies.

[23]Carola Stern, *Porträt einer bolschewistischen Partei* (Köln: Verlag für Politik und Wirtschaft, 1957), pp. 217-18.

5: THE PRESENT STAGE: 1961 AND AFTER

That ugly, but nonetheless effective, engineering exercise known as the Berlin Wall is the backdrop for the present stage. Two of the most important problems facing the German Democratic Republic were rationalizing party and economic organization and stemming the outflow of important segments of the population.[1] The East German response to the thaw had accomplished nothing by way of rallying the people to the purposes and goals of the Socialist Unity Party. Consequently more drastic measures were required if the system were to survive.

Beyond the problems of organization and population, were the severe economic dislocations brought on by the forced collectivization of 1960 and the economic difficulties that hit the rest of the Soviet Bloc at about the same time. The Soviet Union was forced to cut off raw materials on which the East German economy had increasingly come to depend. These factors were combined with chronic labor shortages and inadequate

[1]Consult: "The Trend of Refugees from the Soviet Zone and the Soviet Sector of Berlin," Table compiled by the Federal Ministry for Expellees, Refugees and War Victims (Bonn: 1962), for the relations between events and population movement.

worker productivity. All of this added up to the decision to close the sector boundaries in Berlin.

There were costs and risks associated with the closing of the Berlin sector boundaries. More rigid control of the population, loss of Western trade, and international approbation were among the possible costs: armed conflict was the risk. The costs and the risk turned out to be short-range propositions. The Western powers eliminated the risk by not challenging the construction of the wall. The East German population, cut off from the West and disappointed by Western inaction for a third time after 1953 and 1956, turned to making the best of what was to be had in the G.D.R. This was to have a profound influence on the belief system of East Germany.

Belief System

Basic values and goals. It is useful in discussing the basic values and goals of this period to make a distinction between their internal and external manifestations in the G.D.R. Although the immediate concerns of the SED were with internal problems, it was also concerned with the problem of *Störfreimachung* ("elimination of interference") a synonym for economic independence from the Federal Republic of Germany and the remainder of Western Europe.

Externally Ulbricht was concerned with satisfactory solutions to two important questions: the status of West Berlin and the international recognition of the G.D.R. These became particularly important to the G.D.R., the Soviet Union, and the whole of the communist state system as the Sino-Soviet split widened. Ulbricht's concern with this problem was illustrated by his attempts to exploit the split by courting the Chinese, while at the same time seeking political support from his East European neighbors for his relatively more aggressive position toward the West.[2] Czechoslovakia proved to be the only Bloc country even remotely interested in these attempts, but it did not offer the necessary degree of support.

Ulbricht apparently wanted to exploit the Sino–Soviet split. But the fact that the G.D.R. and the SED were virtually dependent upon the Soviet Union for their existence and that China was in no position to replace Soviet support, underscored the untenability of Ulbricht's policy. As if to prevent such a distant possibility from ever becoming a reality, the Soviet Union undertook to further integrate the G.D.R. within the bloc by co-ordinating industrial development and linking economic plans.[3]

Expectation of goal achievement.   During the time the G.D.R. was making efforts to exploit the Sino–Soviet tensions, the Soviet Union made efforts to consolidate its relationship with Ulbricht and to make clear that such behavior on Ulbricht's part was intolerable. Ulbricht, however, was successful in making his goals known. Both sides appear to have made concessions, with the G.D.R. returning to normally loyal behavior and making some symbolic de-Stalinization gestures.[4] The Berlin Wall probably represents the extent of

[2]Ilse Spittmann, "Achse Pankow-Prag," *SBZ-Archiv,* XIII, no. 11 (June, 1962), 162-64.

[3]Carola Stern, "East Germany," *Communism in Europe,* ed. W. E. Griffeth (Cambridge, Mass.: MIT Press, 1966), II, 115.

[4]Heinz Kersten, "Ostberliner Schriftstellerappell," *SBZ-Archiv,* XIV, no. 7 (April, 1963), 97-98, for an example of "de-Stalinization."

Soviet willingness to alter the status of Berlin. No G.D.R. peace treaty was forthcoming, thus hampering the campaign for international recognition. Even if international goals were largely frustrated, it seems certain that some concessions were made to the East Germans. These very likely took the form of long-range plans and promises in the economic sphere. Ulbricht showed his appreciation by publicly condemning the Chinese.[5] The expectations of goal achievement in the G.D.R., particularly with respect to domestic problems, reached a new high among the leadership after the erection of the Wall.

Cultural orientation.   The cultural orientation of East Germany was not substantially changed subsequent to the building of the Wall. However, a rather careful scrutiny by the Party of the cultural aspects of East German life and a more intensified effort to exercise stricter control over this cultural life does seem to have been initiated. Symptomatic of this were efforts made by the SED to co-ordinate contemporary literature with their program of forced collectivization in 1960-61. Amid accusations that "literature is not keeping pace with life," writers were challenged to live in rural areas, to acquaint themselves with conditions there, and to cast their writings accordingly. A precedent for this and similar demands had been established in 1952, during earlier efforts to collectivize agriculture.[6] Simi-

[5]Günther Nollau, "Der Zerfall der Dritten Internationale," *SBZ-Archiv*, XIV, no. 14 (July, 1963), 216-18; and "SED: Chinesen Erpressen und Spalten," *SBZ-Archiv*, XV, no. 6 (March, 1964), 83-84.

[6]Karl Römer, "Dichter und Bauer auf der Kolchose," *SBZ-Archiv*, XII, no. 11 (June, 1961), 173-75.

lar re-examinations took place in the film industry [7] and in the types of materials made available in East German libraries.[8] However, events with considerable impact upon the cultural sphere did not appear until the Sixth Congress of the Socialist Unity Party in 1963.

The SED had exhibited considerable concern over the artistic liberalization in the neighboring People's Republics, particularly Poland and Hungary, but not excluding the more conservative Czechoslovakia. Although the SED feared undesirable influences, its only measure of control was prohibition. Censorship tended to cut off East German intellectual life from vital movements both Eastern and Western. "Revisionist" works of Soviet or Polish origin were perhaps even less welcome than questionable Western products since they bore a certain legitimacy coming from fraternal socialist neighbors. Ever-present hopes that de-Stalinization in the arts might eventually affect the G.D.R. faded when the Soviet press reported Khrushchev's negative remarks about abstract art at a Moscow art exhibition. Artists were reminded at the Sixth Party Congress that "art, in its totality, is an integral part of ideology." [9]

Religion. The SED has continually concerned itself with both Protestant and Catholic churches. In the past, the Party has been frustrated in its efforts to subdue both institutions by splitting them East and West

[7]Heinz Kersten, "Der Zonenfilm und sein Publikum," *SBZ-Archiv*, XIII, no. 22 (November, 1962), 345-48.

[8]Martin Thilo, *Das Bibliothekswesen in der Sowjetischen Besatzungszone Deutschlands* (Bonn and Berlin: Bundesministerium für Gesamtdeutsche Fragen, 1964).

[9]Heinz Kersten, "Die Defensive der Dogmatiker," *SBZ-Archiv*, XIV, no. 5 (March, 1963), 66-70.

with the goal of ending outside support for "national" churches. The isolated churches would presumably be more amenable to control.

For their part, the churches have attempted to avoid conflict by not responding to political challenges. This, of course, is extremely difficult. One tactic the churches have had to contend with is the official designation of certain churchmen as progressives and others as reactionaries. This effort to split the churches from within was particularly aimed at the individualism of the Protestant Church. This tactic has been unsuccessful, by and large. The Protestant leadership has steadfastly maintained that the church must remain independent from political power.[10]

In the present state there have been renewed efforts by the Party to resolve the church problems. There is evidence that both the Catholic and Protestant churches are making every effort to remain effective without going into a kind of ghetto existence. This is becoming progressively more difficult. In 1963 the Synod of the Protestant Church of Germany, which met in West Germany, was for the first time unattended by representatives from the East. This signaled intensification of the division campaign.

An altogether clear picture of the present situation is hard to bring into focus, partly because of incomplete and contradictory evidence. On the one side is the continued effort to isolate the church in East Germany. On the other are accounts of difficult, but concrete efforts by churchmen to find a place in the socialist order.

[10]Friedhelm Baukloh, "Ulbricht bekommt keine Staatskirche," *SBZ-Archiv*, XII, no. 23 (December, 1961), 364-67.

The moves to isolate the Protestant church have proceeded with the aid of leaders of the eastern Christian Democratic Union (CDU) and with an intensive propaganda campaign by the SED. The campaign branded the all-German Evangelical Church organization as the "NATO church" and denounced the Western church leadership, which has been denied entry into the G.D.R.[11]

Partially successful efforts on the part of churchmen in the G.D.R. to find a *modus vivendi* on which to base their survival are also apparent. A visitor to the G.D.R. reported what may be a typical attitude, although it would seem to reinforce the isolation sought by the regime: "Again and again . . . even people of conservative or bourgeois background told me: 'We disagree with the totalitarian features of present-day socialism, but we are not a fifth column working against it and we will not permit ourselves to be used to trigger a third world war.' "[12] Yet in spite of these views, which have overtones of successful propaganda in them, the eastern CDU is reported to play a role in the G.D.R. which resulted in modifications of the recently passed family law. Moreover, the eastern CDU has intervened to aid maligned individuals. Finally, the finding that baptisms and confirmations have been more numerous since 1964 would indicate that at least the Protestant church is holding its own.[13]

[11]Dietrich Strothmann, "Ulbrichts, was Ulbrichts ist . . .," *Die Zeit* (North American Edition), no. 34 (August 29, 1967).

[12]Markus Barth, "Church and Communism in East Germany: I," *Christian Century*, LXXXIII, no. 47 (November 23, 1966), 1440.

[13]Markus Barth, "Church and Communism in East Germany: II," *Christian Century*, LXXXIII, no. 48 (November 30, 1966), 1472.

THE GERMAN DEMOCRATIC REPUBLIC

Image of self in the world. It is difficult to assess the nature of the self-image of the G.D.R. in the period immediately following construction of the Wall. Certainly the Wall was in part motivated by an intense desire to achieve status in the community of nations through international recognition. Indeed the desperation of these efforts infer a kind of East German inferiority complex. However, as of 1966, the German Democratic Republic had only the following types and distribution of international representation:

Embassies in:

Albania	Mongolia
Bulgaria	Poland
China (People's Republic)	Rumania
Cuba	U.S.S.R.
Czechoslovakia	Vietnam (North)
Hungary	Yugoslavia
Korea (North)	

Consular establishments in:

Burma	Syria
Cambodia	Tanzania
Ceylon	U.A.R.
Indonesia	Yemen
Iraq	

In addition a number of governmental trade missions and offices of the G.D.R. Chamber of International Commerce have been established in countries desirous of trade, but unwilling to recognize the East German government. The foregoing list is hardly a testimony to success in achieving international recognition.

At the same time a certain quality of self-assurance

began manifesting itself after the Wall. At least within the Soviet Bloc, Ulbricht appeared to move with more assurance, as his handling of German policy vis-à-vis the Sino–Soviet split shows. This self-assurance was to increase as the Wall became more of a fixture.

Response patterns to crises. The response patterns to crises appear to differ from those of earlier periods only to the extent that a somewhat greater degree of independence was exhibited by Ulbricht in his dealings with the problems leading to August 13. Whereas earlier responses had been characterized by "turning inward" and resulted in changes within the party structure (New Course, and so forth), the pattern in connection with the crisis produced by the Wall was at least a temporary turn "outward." The reasons for this difference in pattern are difficult to assess, but it seems likely that Ulbricht felt his position had become weakened by the state of things before the Wall. Although the need for change was evident, he was concerned with the possible effect this action might have upon the population at large. Examination in retrospect would seem to at least partially substantiate this likelihood. Following his outward move in the Sino–Soviet interlude, Ulbricht apparently felt ready to push for internal changes following the Wall. In this sense it may be said that he first turned outward and then inward.

A comparison of this with his earlier responses to crises illustrates the overwhelming complexity of both the circumstances surrounding Ulbricht's own political situation as well as those surrounding the political situation of the G.D.R. within the communist system. Despite all measures of institutionalization and integration, there appear to be some areas in which the underlying forces must be carefully and properly assessed before any decisive action may be carried out with any hope of success. The multilevel institutions of the communist system do not appear to have developed to the extent that they may be relied upon as a progressively stabilizing factor over time.

The Social System

Political. Two changes of this period merit special mention. The first involves alterations in the G.D.R. Council of State; the second is the reorganization of the SED according to the "Production Principle," beginning in October, 1962.

The major features of the Council of State have already been outlined. It was not long before major expansions of the responsibilities of the Council took place. According to the "Defense Law" of September, 1961 the Council will, "in case of danger or an attack upon the German Democratic Republic, or in fulfillment of international duties, [declare] a state of emergency," [14] during which parts of the constitution may be suspended.

In addition the Standing Orders of the People's Legislature of November 14, 1963 reflects the expansion of the powers of the Council in that it recognizes the power of the Council to issue binding resolutions and decrees.[15] Furthermore, both the Council of Ministers and the High Court of the G.D.R. are responsible to the Council of State. In essence the Council of State combines the executive, legislative, and judicial powers

[14]Karl Wilhelm Fricke, "Staatsrat und Regierung in der 'DDR,'" revised special issue, *SBZ-Archiv,* XIV, no. 24 (December, 1963), 1.
[15]*Ibid.,* p. 2.

in the G.D.R., and, given his position as Chairman, provides Ulbricht with an extraordinary instrument of central control.[16]

The reorganization of the Socialist Unity Party according to the "Production Principle" followed a similar move in the Soviet Union and went into effect at the Sixth Party Congress in January, 1963. The changeover is an example of continual gearing of the SED to the CPSU. More important, the reorganization came at a time when the SED was desperately trying to enhance its economic position with a thoroughgoing reorganization.

Walter Ulbricht had announced at the seventeenth meeting of the SED Central Committee that "certain structural changes in the work of the party-direction were pending" and that "certain forms and methods were outdated," necessitating changes. The basis for the changes was the Politburo decision that the Production Principle, which had been applied to economic organization, "was also applicable in the work and structure of the executive organs of the Party." [17] What this meant was that the SED would be organized from top to bottom according to economic sectors rather than in regional units. At the top bureaus for Industry and Construction and for Agriculture, along with commissions for Agitation and Propaganda, were added under the direction of the Politiburo and the Secretariat of the Central Committee. The two bureaus were to combine technical concerns with ideological considerations in dealing with the economic system, particu-

[16]Siegfried Mampel, *Die Entwicklung der Verfassungsordnung in der sowjetisch besetzten Zone Deutschlands von 1945 bis 1963* [Tübingen: J.C.B. Mohr (Paul Siebeck), 1964], p. 538.

[17]Hans Schimanski, "Parteiaufbau nach Produktionsprinzip," *SBZ-Archiv*, XIV, no. 8 (April, 1963), 119-22.

larly as the New Economic System got underway in the first six months of 1963. The commissions for Agitation and Ideology had existed prior to the reorganization, but in their continuation they were to play a clearly subordinate role in the application of the Production Principle.

Threatened in the reorganization were the party organs at the middle and lower levels (the guts of the party, as it were). With preferences now given to the industrial technicians, engineers, and economists in the SED, the party hack saw his position seriously undermined. It appears that the threat was real and part of a conscious effort at upgrading the quality of party functionaries—presumably those surviving would be the most competent. In addition it was hoped that the reorganization would bring the party closer to the people, thereby helping to close the gap between the public and the party apparatus.

The threatened party cadre was not without resources. And before the passage of a year a re-emphasis on the territorial organizations was noticeable.[18] The young technocrats had a difficult task in attempting to outmaneuver the hard-line "dogmatists." Slowly but surely the balance swung back to the needs of party discipline and a re-emphasis on the work of the commissions for Agitation and Ideology. This is not to say that a full restoration has taken place, but the technocrats have been shown definite limits.

Economic. The initial thrust after the Wall was for economic independence from the West. This was part of a general campaign aimed at cutting off all Western

[18]P. C. Ludz, "Produktionsprinzip versus Territorialprinzip," *SBZ-Archiv*, XVI, nos. 1-2 (January, 1965), 5.

influences such as radio and TV beamed from the Federal Republic and West Berlin.

Owing to the structure of prewar trade between the areas of East and West Germany, with the West providing important raw materials such as coal and steel and with the East supplying rather less crucial finished products, the G.D.R. might well have felt something of an economic threat should the Federal Republic arbitrarily choose to stop trading. East-West trade had been expanding in the decade before 1961. Although 1961 itself shows the expected drop in trade between the G.D.R. and the Federal Republic,[19] more recently there has been a return to pre-Wall levels; 1964 showed an all time high in the volume of trade in spite of difficulties in negotiating satisfactory agreements between the trading partners.[20] This kind of development is hard for the political leaderships of East and West to bear ideologically, particularly since there are persistent internal pressures on both sides for further increases.[21]

The effort to free itself economically from any kind of dependence on the West was clearly not a solution to the economic problems facing the G.D.R. What was indicated for East German economic ills was a deep-reaching reorganization of the economy and this was the aim of the New Economic System for Planning and Directing the National Economy.

The East German New Economic System (NES) has had considerable significance for the economies of the

[19]Karel Holbik and Henry Myers, *Postwar Trade in Divided Germany* (Baltimore: The Johns Hopkins Press, 1964), pp. 61-62.
[20]*SBZ von A-Z* (Bonn: Deutscher Bundesverlag, 1966), p. 216.
[21]Holbik and Myers, *Postwar Trade in Divided Germany,* pp. 106-10.

Soviet Bloc as an example and an experiment. Three areas deserve special attention. First, the G.D.R. led the Bloc in taking up the "Liberman discussion" and translating it into an ongoing economy. Second, the NES offered the East Germans a way out of the chaos that underlay its "planned" economy. And finally, the experience of the New Economic System in the G.D.R. seems to have described the limits of political and economic interaction in a communist system at the East German stage of development.

Professor Liberman of Kharkov began a Bloc-wide discussion in September, 1962, when he proposed a series of reforms that would decentralize control over production and introduce the concepts of price, profit, interest, and value, based on something approaching a competitive market. Liberman set the tone by writing:

It is necessary to find a sufficiently simple and at the same time reasonable solution for one of the main tasks that has been put forward by the program of the CPSU: to develop a system of planning and evaluating the performance of enterprises in such a way as to mobilize their self-interest in the highest possible planning targets, in introducing new techniques, in improving the quality of products—in a word, in the highest possible efficiency of production.[22]

The implications of these thoughts in both the economic and political sectors were profound, as indicated by the intensity of the debate following the publication of Liberman's ideas. Economically, the revisions, if

[22]Karl C. Thalheim, "The Development of the East German Economy in the Framework of the Soviet Bloc," *Eastern Europe in Transition,* ed. Kurt London (Baltimore: The Johns Hopkins Press, 1966), p. 161.

effected, would lead to an overhauling of a "command economy" with an attendant loss of political control. Relatively few of the reform suggestions were introduced in the Soviet Union. And many of the reforms that were adopted were nullified after Khrushchev's ouster in 1964.

In spite of the controversy and contrary to its reputation as one of the more conservative members of the Bloc, the German Democratic Republic moved quickly in the fall of 1962 to put their New Economic System into effect beginning in July, 1963. The rapidity of the adoption, which required frenzied activity on the part of the East German economic functionaries, is evidence that the G.D.R. leadership recognized that the construction of the Wall had solved only one of the two basic problems for which it was designed. That is, although the population had been numerically stabilized since August 13, 1961, the economy had not.

Fritz Schenk has summarized the instability of the East German economy by counting the failures of the various plans:

For practical purposes the Zone has had no economic perspective for five years and it has been ten years since a perspective-plan has been realized. The First Five Year Plan (1951-1955), even if it was changed several times, was at least officially concluded. The Second Five Year Plan (1956-1960) was one and one-half years late as a law and was broken off six months later. The first Seven Year Plan (1959-1965) was presented as a law—the Federal Republic should be passed and surpassed—but had to be recognized as a failure by the SED in 1961 and given up in 1962. For 1963 there was a transitional plan. From 1964 on the second Seven Year Plan was scheduled to run (1964-1970). Thus far only the directive of the Sixth Party Congress of

1963 has appeared. A plan law has not appeared in the intervening three years.[23]

Indeed the ineffectuality evident in trying to make a planned economy work in East Germany is evidence that the system was ready for a change, that the planned style was no longer the effective one for the stage of economic development that the G.D.R. had reached.[24] According to this view, developed by James Elliott and Anthony Scaperlanda, the East German economy following the war was essentially underdeveloped because the "use of available technology was retarded" under the aegis of a command economy. The dynamics of the economy, however, moves it to a stage in which "a higher and more complex level of technology yields a relatively high per capita product." At this point a market type of economy is more appropriate in the sense of most efficiently utilizing the potential of the level of technological development. Furthermore, the kinds of skills, both technological and economic, that a developed and developing economy needs, produce the kinds of people that are likely to press for changes in organization. These people, the young technocrats, came to the fore in 1962-63.

Ulbricht gave the young technocrats their way in reforming the East German economy. These party and state functionaries in their thirties and forties introduced elements into the economy that were hardly understood by the older "apparatchiki." Their wrath was instant. Yet under the umbrella of Ulbricht's pa-

[23]Fritz Schenk, "Die zweite Etappe der Planlosigkeit," *SBZ-Archiv*, XVII, nos. 1-2 (January, 1966), 1.

[24]James R. Elliott and Anthony E. Scaperlanda, "East Germany's Liberman-type Reforms in Perspective," *The Quarterly Review of Economics and Business*, VI, no. 3 (Autumn, 1966), 41.

tronage the New Economic System was previewed at the Sixth Party Congress in January, 1963, and put into effect six months later.

In producing the New Economic System the younger functionaries drew on all the enthusiasm and training at their command. Indeed the élan and optimism of the first months of the NES were infectious. Some of the flavor of the period can be sampled in Wolfgang Berger's "The New Economic System in the G.D.R.—Its Essence and Problems," which appeared in the *World Marxist Review* for February, 1965: "It is gratifying to see energetic, capable young people coming to the fore. Graduates of the technical and economic colleges, too young to have been bogged down in the old administrative practices have shown themselves capable of coping with challenging problems." [25]

In addition to their own capacities and enthusiasm, the new economic leadership had help from the files of private capital. The American concerns nationalized by Cuba provided a storehouse of information for the economics specialists of the G.D.R.[26]

What does the New Economic System look like? [27] Figure 1 shows the basic configuration of the East German economy as of 1966. The simplicity of the pattern is somewhat misleading in that it does not show the

[25]Wolfgang Berger, "The New Economic System in the G.D.R. —Its Essence and Problems," *World Marxist Review,* VIII, no. 2 (February, 1965), 13.

[26]D. Bandis *et al.,* "Aus den Geheimarchiven amerikanischer Monopole in Kuba: Die Planung bei Standard Oil (1957 bis 1960)," *Jahrbuch für Wirtschaftsgeschichte, 1966,* pt. III (East Berlin: Akademie Verlag, 1966), pp. 11-32.

[27]For a more complete description of the NES plan see: *Das funktionelle Wirken der Bestandteile des neuen ökonomischen Systems der Planung und Leitung der Volkswirtschaft* (East Berlin: Dietz Verlag, 1964).

processes of economic planning with which the New Economic System was designed to deal.

The planning chaos has already been described. Beneath the confusion lay a stagnating economy. Following the rapid growth of the East German economy in the mid-1950s a period of slow growth, characteristic of the Soviet Bloc economies at the time, complicated the immediate impact of forced collectivization in 1961 and the post-Wall readjustments.

The NES was supposed to eliminate the stultifying effects of long-range planning, the inflexibility of which did not allow industry to take advantage of unplanned changes in conditions. Also to be eliminated were the detailed, short-run plans that led plant managers to concentrate on goal fulfillment rather than on efficiency. In order to achieve the former, perspective-planning was to replace multiyear plans. In 1965 it was announced that only the broadest guidelines would be provided and that the burden of planning would devolve from the then dissolved National Economic Council to the Associations of People's Industries (VVB). In place of the National Economic Council, the Industrial Ministries (shown in Fig. 1) would provide the intermediary link between the State Planning Commission and the VVB.

To wean plant managers away from the temptations of fulfilling plan objectives at any cost, the notions of price, profit, investment, and cost accounting were introduced by the New Economic System. The Associations of People's Industries and the managers of the People's Enterprises (VEB) now would be judged on the basis of cost and efficiency per unit rather than on numbers or tonnage. Furthermore, with the introduction of the concept of a socialist market, the managers

Fig. 1. The Economy of the G.D.R. (1966)

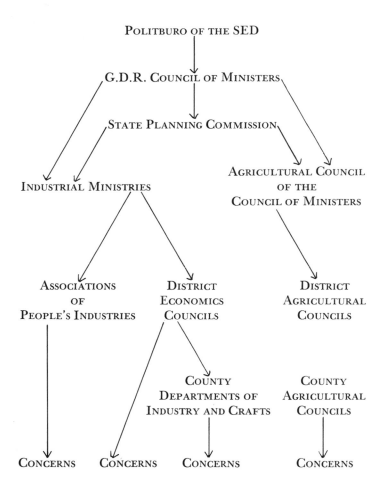

Adapted from: SBZ von A-Z (1966), p. 538.

had to sell what they produced either at home to consumers who were getting richer and more selective or abroad where meeting the "world standard" would be the measure of success or failure. Finally, the plant managers were made subject to and given a system of economic levers or incentives. Bonuses for plan fulfillment under the New Economic System were made contingent on efficiency. The salaries of top management and even those of the middle range were linked to the efficiency of the operation. Plants were charged "interest on capital," encouraging prudent investment and capital utilization.

The NES in operation shows some eighty Associations of People's Industries supervising the work of over 1,500 enterprises that account for two-thirds of the industrial output of the German Democratic Republic. Within this complex all has not gone smoothly. Although it is much too early to judge success or failure, some of the limits of the New Economic System have become apparent.

The limitations on the NES are political, economic, and international in the sense of bloc integration. Mention has been made of the sensitivity of the party bureaucrats to the importance accorded the young technocrats led by the head of the State Planning Commission, Erich Apel. The technicians, who had been given their way by Ulbricht at the Sixth Party Congress of 1963, were reined in by the conservatives at the Eleventh Plenum of the SED meeting in December, 1965, shortly after Apel's suicide.[28]

The changes made at the Eleventh Plenum took away some of the authority of the General Directors of

[28]Ilse Spittmann, "East Germany: The Swinging Pendulum," *Problems of Communism*, XVI, no. 4 (July-August, 1967), 14.

the Associations of People's Enterprises. The National Economic Council, which the General Directors had been under, was eliminated and in its stead they were made responsible to the Industrial Ministries. Furthermore, all plan proposals were to be submitted to the ministries prior to being passed to the State Planning Commission. Finally the self-audit of the Associations was eliminated.[29] These provisions meant that the Directors, who had been Apel's men, were not going to be their own men.

The conservative trend in the G.D.R. has not wiped out all the changes made in the economic system. What has been eliminated are the hopes that a victory of the young technocrats would bring in its train a progressive liberalization. Even though Ulbricht appointed seventeen new ministers in 1965, of whom only one was over 45 years old, the conflict between young and old has not produced a liberalization in the Party. It is this liberalization that is crucial, for it is in the latent conflict between the state bureaucracy and the party apparatus that the liberalism–conservatism issue will be decided. And it seems "that the numerically superior, but in their political influence meaningless stratum of young professionals in the Zone, as in the Soviet Union, do not appear to have won the upper hand. Moving up strongly, however, are the Party cadre. These deserve our attention."[30] The 35 to 45 age group in the SED leadership is pictured as tough and hard, forged in the harsh years of the Stalinist order. As long as this group remains in control, a line

[29]P. C. Ludz, "East Germany: The Old and the New," *East Europe,* XV, no. 4 (April, 1966), 26.

[30]Fritz Schenk, "Die Enkel der Revolution," *SBZ-Archiv,* XVII, no. 23 (December, 1966), 357-58.

more dogmatic than liberal can be expected.[31] If this is the case, then the political system will continue to set the economic experts rigid limits.

Economic problems have done their share in holding back the development of the New Economic System. The transition from one kind of economic order to another brings with it enormous strains. The introduction of prices related to a market mechanism has meant upsetting expectations. Most of these expectations were based on prices for power and raw materials that were below those that a market would set. This was a means by which subventions were made in a planned economy. When some higher prices were asked and others were bid up by competing managers of the People's Enterprises, a wave of dislocations went through the economy. Others were felt when cost accounting was introduced and when a kind of interest on capital was charged.

The result, in the economic sphere, might be described as a "neither–nor" system. Decentralization in planning was not accompanied by freedom from centralized decision making. A full market economy, even in the socialist sense, has not been forthcoming. And lack of adequate financing remains a block in the way of a full realization of the NES.

The demands made on the East Germans by the integrative tendencies within the Soviet Bloc prevented the New Economic System from fully realizing its potential in the world market. A series of more or less well defined phases in the international development of the G.D.R. economy can be seen as:

[31]For a comprehensive study of the East German political elite see P. C. Ludz, *Parteielite im Wandel* (Köln and Opladen: Westdeutscher Verlag, 1968).

1. Autarky from 1949 to 1954. During this stage the concentration was on internal economic development.
2. COMECON from 1954 to the early 1960s. With the end to reparations came the integration into the system of communist states.
3. World Market from the early to mid-1960s. The NES sought, in its initial phases, to trade with both East and West.
4. COMECON-Soviet Union from 1966 to present.[32]

This return to dependence on the Soviet Union followed a series of events in the fall of 1965, beginning with negotiations leading to a renewal of the G.D.R.–U.S.S.R. trade pact and ending on December 3, the day Erich Apel committed suicide.

Although the official East German versions explain Apel's suicide as a result of strain and overwork in the case of the New Economic System, it is more likely that he was despondent over the outcome of negotiations with the Soviet Union which led to a renewal of the mutual trade agreement.[33] Talks had begun in Moscow during the preceding September. Soviet demands were high in that low prices on finished products were being asked without compensating reductions in raw materials provided by the Soviet Union. Furthermore, the Soviets wanted the delivery of goods promised earlier but never delivered by the G.D.R.

Ordinarily the expectation would have been for immediate East German acquiescence. However, the G.D.R. delegation returned to Berlin without reaching

[32]Manfred Rexin, "Recent Reforms in East Germany," *World Today,* XXI, no. 7 (July, 1965), 303.

[33]Welles Hangen, *The Muted Revolution* (New York: Alfred Knopf, 1966), pp. 3-5.

a final agreement. Negotiations bogged down. It took a visit to Berlin by Leonid Brezhnev at the end of November to secure the East German signature finally ordered by Ulbricht. The pact was signed hours after Apel's death.

The trade pact returning the G.D.R. to the fold of COMECON and the Soviet Union, the economic complications of transition, and the political demands of the SED party bureaucracy have not combined to put an end to the New Economic System. However its potential has been inhibited. Michael Gamarnikow summed up the situation with regard to the NES in the German Democratic Republic as:

quite in keeping with German industrial tradition [and] may eventually develop a *dirigiste* economy, dominated by large quasi-monopolistic and semi-independent concerns— the Vereinigungen Volkseigener Betriebe. The East German party leadership is carrying out its own reforms according to its own schedule, without any of the popular pressure which is such an important factor elsewhere in the bloc. And the Ulbricht regime shows no intention of surrendering the essentials of its tight control over the economy.[34]

Education. The Socialist Unity Party feels that the G.D.R. is now in the phase of "Comprehensive Construction of Socialism." In moving toward the achievement of the status of a fully socialist order, education has played a prominent role. As was pointed out earlier, educational reforms have had as prime elements the training of socialist citizens and the provision of the greatest variety of educational opportunities to

[34]Michael Gamarnikow, "The Reforms: A Survey," *East Europe,* XV, no. 1 (January, 1966), 17.

people of all backgrounds. In 1965 the Law on the Unified Socialist Educational System was passed by the Volkskammer, acting on the results of a two-year debate begun at the Sixth Party Congress of January, 1963. The timing of the debate and resulting law are not coincidentally related to the New Economic System. Although there was a tendency at the time to talk about everything in the G.D.R. in terms of the NES, the new developments in education were definitely linked to the economic system, as indeed they had been since the reforms of 1959. This was especially the case because of the concentration on the economics and sociology of education after 1961.[35]

The 1965 law is not revolutionary in character. Rather it consolidates the experiences of earlier educational reforms and tries to deal with some of the problems that have haunted East German education.[36] Figure 2 presents a schematic of the G.D.R. educational system. The problems included within this system and which it is designed to deal with include the need for better preparation in mathematics and natural sciences, the inability of students to acquire knowledge on their own, inadequate capacity to handle the language, and insufficient political–ideological training. With the exception of the last, the problems could be those of nearly any Western educational system.

The essential difference between the educational system of the G.D.R. and those of Western societies lies in the state control over the student from his earliest years through the university. This tends to

[35]P. C. Ludz, "Bildungsökonomie und Bildungssoziologie," *SBZ-Archiv,* XVI, no. 17 (September, 1965), 262-66.
[36]Manfred Rexin, "Von der Kinderkrippe zur Universität," *SBZ-Archiv,* XVI, nos. 11-12 (June, 1965), 171-75.

Fig. 2. The Educational System of the G.D.R.

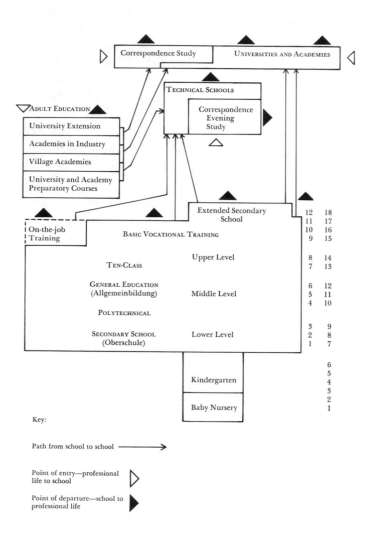

Key:

Path from school to school ⟶

Point of entry—professional
life to school ▷

Point of departure—school to
professional life ▶

Adapted from: SBZ von A-Z (1966), p. 129.

102

keep the individual's behavior in the public sector. Furthermore, the G.D.R. school system is designed to integrate the individual into the productive process as rapidly as possible and provides for leaving school at the end of eight years with educational completion on the job.

The educational system of the G.D.R. has been used to modify the East German class structure, first by denying education to the children of the middle and upper classes following the war and then by making opportunities available on the broadest base. This is one of the changes in the G.D.R. that has had far-reaching influence and that has supported Ralf Dahrendorf's thesis that the East German state is the "first modern society on German soil." [37]

Military. In considering political and economic developments in East Germany the military is often overlooked. A major concern is with the reliability of the National People's Army (NVA). Since the construction of the Wall much has been made of troop defections to the West. In fact, since 1952 some 30,000 troops have deserted. This would seem to indicate unreliability. At the same time the East German military establishment seems to be increasing in importance within the Warsaw Pact and the NVA is becoming a reliable force.

In 1963 General Heinz Hoffmann, once a battalion commander of the Eleventh International Brigade during the Spanish Civil War, commanded Soviet, Polish, Czech, and German forces in joint war games. This was the first time a German officer had been ac-

[37]Ralf Dahrendorf, *Gesellschaft und Demokratie in Deutschland* (Munich: Piper & Co. Verlag, 1965), p. 453.

THE GERMAN DEMOCRATIC REPUBLIC

corded this honor. The military establishment that
General Hoffmann oversees as G.D.R. Minister of
National Defense is modern and well-equipped, and
the NVA "has often received new items of equipment
sooner than any of the other East European communist armies." [38] The command and the equipment
suggest a certain amount of trust and confidence as well
as necessity as the NVA operates within the framework
of Soviet Bloc military strategy.

Recent assessments by military commentators agree
that at a minimum the NVA would be reliable as a
fighting force if "sandwiched in between or in front of
Soviet forces." [39] More recently L. J. M. van den Berk
has said: "The original scorn of the soldiers for any
military organization and their suspicion that the
armed forces might be employed against the Federal
Republic of Germany are being increasingly thrust
into the background by a certain pride in mastery of
the military craft and in not being inferior to the
soldiers of other countries. A sort of German Democratic Republic consciousness has developed." [40]

It is interesting to note that, although the NVA has
relied on conscription since 1962, only the Soviet Bloc
military establishment makes provision for alternative
service for conscientious objectors. This service, made
available in 1964, is in *Baueinheiten* ("construction
units") of the NVA. Even though these units have no
weapons and their members need swear no military

[38]R. L. Garthoff, "The Military Establishment," *East Europe,*
XIV, no. 9 (September, 1965), 11.

[39]James T. Reitz, "The Satellite Armies . . . A Soviet Asset?,"
Military Review, XLV, no. 10 (October, 1965), 33.

[40]L. J. M. van den Berk, "Military Developments in Poland,
Czechoslovakia, and East Germany," *Military Review,* XLVI, no,
12 (December, 1966), 52.

oath of loyalty, it is clear that this form of service is not acceptable to many pacifists.[41] However, that the East German regime would go even this far in meeting demands that must have come primarily from the Protestant church is indicative of sensitivity to group demands in the G.D.R. even after August 13.

[41]David Childs, "The 'Nationale Volksarmee' of East Germany," *German Life & Letters,* New Series, XX, no. 3 (April, 1967), 195-204.

6: EVALUATION: TRENDS AND PROSPECTS

After the end of World War II a truncated Germany was further subdivided into four zones of occupation. Each of the four occupying powers had its own notions about the future of Germany. It was not long before it became apparent that co-operation among the occupiers would be limited to the zones associated with the leaders of an emerging bipolar world. The Soviet blockade of the land routes to Berlin in 1948 gave impetus to a process whereby the eastern and western parts of Germany were taken into the systems of the communist party states and the North Atlantic Area.

Postwar Germany presents a case of two distinct political systems emerging from a common cultural base. Each system is developing within the framework of associated states with similarly developing political and economic systems. The degree of integration of the east and west German states can be roughly measured by the extent to which the two differ in a variety of aspects. Three measures that indicate the sort of differentiation that can help appraise the state of G.D.R. integration within the communist party state system are industrial standards, language, and elite change.

In a subtle way the German language as used in the

Federal Republic and the G.D.R. is changing differentially. It would be a gross exaggeration to say that two languages have developed.[1] Nonetheless, there are increasing areas in which the same words have taken on such various meanings that some amount of translation is necessary.[2] One example among many is the recently published *Philosophisches Wörterbuch,* which proclaims itself the "first of its kind built on a Marxist-Leninist base."[3] The presentation is premised on the works of Marx, Engels, and Lenin, plus the basic documents of the SED and CPSU. Insofar as the *Wörterbuch* serves as a guide to usage in the G.D.R. (and as a guide to understanding for the outsider), a whole new philosophical vocabulary has been and is being evolved in the G.D.R. that represents a break with the German cultural tradition carried on in the Federal Republic—even though Marx and Engels are parts of the German cultural tradition per se.[4]

Changes in the elite structures of postwar Germany also indicate that the political and social orders of East and West have undergone considerable change.[5] This

[1] Hugo Moser, *Sprachliche Folgen der politischen Teilung Deutschlands* (Düsseldorf: Pädagogischer Verlag Schwann, 1962), pp. 48-49.

[2] Ernst G. Riemschneider, *Veränderungen der deutschen Sprache in der sowjetisch besetzten Zone Deutschlands seit 1945* (Düsseldorf: Pädagogischer Verlag Schwann, 1963).

[3] Georg Klaus and Manfred Burr, eds., *Philosophisches Wörterbuch* (Leipzig: VEB Bibliographisches Institut, 1964), p. v.

[4] This point, which is frequently overlooked, is emphasized by Jean Edward Smith, "The German Democratic Republic and the West," *International Journal,* XXII, no. 2 (Spring, 1967), 231-52.

[5] Wolfgang Zapf, "Führungsgruppen in Ost und West," *Beiträge zur Analyse der deutschen Oberschicht,* ed. W. Zapf (Munich: Piper & Co. Verlag, 1965), pp. 9-29.

holds not only for current East-West comparisons, but for earlier periods as well. For example, an examination of legislative elites of the Weimar Reichstag, the Bundestag of the Federal Republic, and the G.D.R. Volkskammer showed the following features:

Age:	Weimar	— preponderantly middle age
	West	— preponderantly old age
	East	— preponderantly young
Education:	Weimar	— bimodal distribution of high and low
	West	— high level of education
	East	— relatively even distribution
Occupation:	Weimar	— professions and "interests" dominant
	West	— professions and bureaucrats dominant
	East	— relatively even distribution of professions, party functionaries, and "interests" [6]

These reflect the impact of educational reforms, comparative accents on age groups, and groupings within the societies.

Industrial standards setting such basic items as paper sizes and gauges came under the purview of the

[6]A. M. Hanhardt, Jr., and Randal L. Cruikshanks, "Legislative Representatives and Social Change: Reichstag, Bundestag and Volkskammer," (unpublished manuscript, University of Oregon, 1967), p. 7.

Deutsche Industrie-Normen (DIN). These standards were continued in postwar Germany with an all-German commission sitting in Berlin to supervise standards in the Federal Republic and the G.D.R. Increasingly in the postwar period, the Soviet Union made deliveries to the G.D.R. in terms of Soviet *Gost-norms*. This compelled the G.D.R. to convert to standards that deviated from the DIN. In the aftermath of the Berlin Wall, the G.D.R. stopped participating in the work of the commission. A systematic conversion program based on DDR-*Standards* (TGL) effectively eliminated compulsory DIN standards in 1962.[7]

Language and industrial standards are symbolic of trends within the developing communist system of the G.D.R. which indicate continuing commitment to and integration within the communist party state system. Indeed the reaction to the most serious case of revisionism in the G.D.R. since the Harich heresy of 1956 —the lectures of Professor Robert Havemann—indicates a maturation of the G.D.R. system behind its Wall. Havemann, whose utopian interpretation of Marxism–Leninism has an almost Chinese purity about it, challenged the ideological foundation of the SED in lectures at the Humboldt University of East Berlin. The SED leadership expelled Havemann from the Party, removed him from his Chair in Physical Chemistry, and dropped him from membership in the Academy of Sciences. But the State Security Service was not called into play, nor was Havemann arrested and tried.[8] This reaction, though sharp considering

[7]*Statistisches Jahrbuch der DDR 1964,* p. 191 and chart facing p. 193.

[8]For an excellent discussion of the Havemann Affair see: P. C. Ludz, "Freiheitsphilosophie oder aufgeklärter Dogmatismus? Zum Denken Robert Havemanns," *SBZ-Archiv,* XV, no. 12 (June, 1964), 183-89 and no. 13 (July, 1964), 195-202.

Havemann's long commitment to the communist cause and his international reputation as a scientist, indicates a surety on the part of the SED that was absent in previous eruptions of revisionism.

Given this surety, the prospect is for a continuation of the present stage with minor internal changes consonant with a modestly but increasingly affluent industrialized communist society. This appears to be particularly the case in view of the findings of Hans Apel.[9] Apel set out to investigate the contention in the Federal Republic that "90% of the residents of the Soviet Zone are opponents of the regime." In what appears to be an unusually careful, one-man survey over time, Apel interviewed East Germans in 1962, 1964, and 1966.

Far from finding East Germans preponderantly opponents of the regime, Apel discovered the distribution displayed in Table 13. This would indicate that support for the social and political order of the German Democratic Republic is sizable and growing. This corroborates the observations of journalists and others that feelings of loyalty and even affect for the state are more widespread than is usually expected in the West.[10]

[9]Hans Apel, "Wie sie es sehen," *Der Monat,* XIX, no. 222 (March, 1967), 15-23; and Apel, "Bericht über das 'Staatsgefühl' der DDR-Bevölkerung," *Frankfurter Hefte,* XXII, no. 3 (March, 1967), 169-78.

[10]See, for example: Peter Frigge, "Citizen, State and Government in East Germany," *Swiss Review of World Affairs,* XVII, no. 3 (June, 1967), 7-9: "An examination of present conditions leads to the conclusion that the idea of a clear-cut popular rejection of the regime by the people, an unequivocal antagonism between those governing and the majority of those governed is now obsolete. . . . No visitor can escape the recognition of how the mood within this Communist state and the attitude toward it have changed. . . ." (p. 7) Similar observations can be found in: Welles Hangen, *The Muted Revolution* (New York: Alfred Knopf, 1966).

It is questionable whether feelings of sufficient intensity are present to speak of an East German nationality to accompany the recent law ending unified German citizenship in favor of the "State Citizen of the G.D.R." [11] Yet it must be recognized that changes are taking place, changes that are widening the gap between the G.D.R. and the Federal Republic.

Relations between East and West Germany during the past year have had the effect of accelerating some integrative tendencies in the G.D.R. As the policy of the Federal Republic toward the G.D.R. and Eastern Europe has become less rigid, Ulbricht has reacted by seeking reassurances from the bloc partners. Following the Federal Republic's establishment of diplomatic relations with Rumania, the fear of becoming isolated in the bloc led to the conclusion of pacts of Friendship and Mutual Assistance with Poland and Czechoslovakia. [12] These treaties followed much the same pattern set by the G.D.R.–U.S.S.R. agreement of June, 1964.

The 1964 treaty with the Soviet Union underlined the co-operative relations of the U.S.S.R. and East Germany within the context of COMECON. And expectations point to a closeness of Soviet, Polish, Czech, and East German relations, reversing the slight downward trend in Soviet trade (from 49.3 to 43.4 per cent of total trade) between 1962 and 1965 and the accompanying Soviet Bloc decline (from 78 to 73.7 per cent) in 1963 and 1964. [13]

Prospects for the future of the G.D.R. must end

[11] Jens Hacker, "Die Zerstörung der deutschen Rechtseinheit," *SBZ-Archiv,* XVIII, no. 5 (March, 1967), 66.

[12] Jens Hacker, "Beistandspakte mit Warschau und Prag," *SBZ-Archiv,* XVIII, no. 6 (March, 1967), 81.

[13] Ilse Spittmann, "East Germany: The Swinging Pendulum," *Problems of Communism,* XVI, no. 4 (July-August, 1967), 16.

with a consideration of the "after Ulbricht" question. Certainly the liberalization from 1963 to 1965 showed a certain trend toward the world markets, toward openness in dealing with problems of ideology and culture. These trends were allowed and even encouraged by Ulbricht and they were ended by Ulbricht. However, it should be emphasized that the liberalization trends stayed within the limits of a modern communist system. The prospects, then, are for a continuation on course, even if Ulbricht is no longer at the helm. This is even more the case when Ulbricht's possible successors are taken into account. There is no one among the hopefuls who has the qualities of leadership and authority to move the German Democratic Republic far from its present place in the formation of the communist party state system.

APPENDIX: SELECTED DATA TABLES

TABLE 1. The East German Share
of the Production of Raw Materials, Energy,
and Manufacturers in 1936 Germany[1]

Product	Percent
Iron-ore mining	5.1
Copper-ore mining	92.8
Coal mining	2.3
Brown coal mining	64.1
Oil production	0.02
Chemical-technical industry[2]	24.0
Electro-energy[3]	33.8
Machine construction[4]	31.3
Including: Machine tools[5]	37.9
Textile machinery	54.3
Agricultural machinery	22.2
Vehicle construction	27.5
Precision tool manufacturing and optical industry	33.1
Clothing industry	44.9
Consumer goods and luxuries industry	31.9

[1]Territorial status of 1957, including the Saarland.
[2]Without Berlin.
[3]1939, without Berlin.
[4]Including vehicle construction, ship building, and airplane industry.
[5]Without Berlin.
Source: Gerhard Schmidt-Renner, ed., *Wirtschaftsterritorium Deutsche Demokratische Republik,* 3rd ed. (East Berlin: Verlag Die Wirtschaft, 1961), p. 23.

TABLE 2. Age Groups in the East German Population

Year	Under 15	Persons of Working Age	Persons of Retirement Age (Men–65 and over; Women–60 and over)
	(%)	(%)	(%)
1946	24.5	62.5	13.0
1950	22.9	63.3	13.8
1951	22.4	63.2	14.4
1952	22.1	63.1	14.8
1953	21.7	63.1	15.2
1954	21.3	63.2	15.1
1955	20.9	63.2	15.9
1956	20.6	63.0	16.4
1957	20.6	62.6	16.8
1958	20.5	62.3	17.2
1959	20.8	61.9	17.3
1960	21.4	61.0	17.6
1961	23.6	58.5	17.9
1962	24.3	57.6	18.1
1963	25.0	56.8	18.2
1964	23.8	57.8	18.4

Source: SBZ von A-Z (1966), p. 83.

TABLE 3. Female Employment in the G.D.R.

Year	Total Labor Force	Female Portion of Total	
		(000's)	(%)
1950	7,196	2,880	40.0
1955	7,722	3,396	44.0
1960	7,739	3,478	44.9
1965	7,676	3,581	46.87

Source: Statistisches Jahrbuch der DDR 1966, p. 23.

TABLE 4. 1965 Populations of Districts

District	Area	Population December 31, 1965	Population Density
	(sq. km.)		*(per sq. km.)*
Rostock	7,072	842,743	119
Schwerin	8,672	594,786	69
Neubrandenburg	10,793	633,209	59
Potsdam	12,569	1,127,498	90
Frankfurt	7,186	660,666	92
Cottbus	8,262	839,133	102
Magdeburg	11,525	1,323,644	115
Halle	8,771	1,932,733	220
Erfurt	7,348	1,249,540	170
Gera	4,004	735,175	184
Suhl	3,856	549,398	142
Dresden	6,738	1,887,739	280
Leipzig	4,966	1,510,773	304
Karl-Marx-Stadt	6,009	2,082,927	347
Berlin (East)	403	1,077,969	2,675
G.D.R.	108,174	17,047,933	158

Source: *Statistisches Jahrbuch der DDR 1966,* p. 3.

TABLE 5. Populations of Selected Communities

Community	Population				
	May 17, 1939	Oct. 29, 1946	Aug. 31, 1950	Dec. 31, 1962	Dec. 31, 1964
Berlin (East)	1,588,262	1,174,582	1,189,074	1,061,218	1,071,462
Cottbus	55,509	49,131	60,874	69,472	73,257
Dresden	630,216	467,966	494,187	494,588	503,859
Eisenhüttenstadt (ex-Stalinstadt)	—	—	—	34,585	36,619
Erfurt	165,615	174,633	188,650	188,452	189,770
Frankfurt (Oder)	83,669*	51,577	52,822	57,669	58,006
Gera	83,375	89,212	98,576	102,959	106,841
Halle (Saale)	220,092	222,505	289,119	278,049	274,402
Karl-Marx-Stadt (ex-Chemnitz)	337,657	250,188	293,373	287,400	293,549
Leipzig	707,365	607,655	617,574	587,226	595,203
Magdeburg	336,838	236,326	260,305	265,512	265,141
Neubrandenburg	21,854	20,446	22,412	37,555	37,934
Potsdam	135,892	113,568	118,180	115,257	109,867
Rostock	121,192	114,869	133,109	166,456	179,352
Schwerin	64,614	88,164	93,576	93,830	91,210
Suhl	23,549	24,598	24,020	26,077	28,177

*Including the sector of the city now in the People's Republic of Poland.
Source: *Statistisches Jahrbuch der DDR 1965*, pp. 11-13.

TABLE 6. Internal Migration, 1963

Size of Community	Immigration:	Gain or Loss
to 2,000	—	51,074
2,000 to 5,000	—	7,314
5,000 to 10,000	+	3,850
10,000 to 20,000	+	10,012
20,000 to 50,000	+	9,845
50,000 to 100,000	+	9,188
100,000 and over	+	25,493

Source: Petermanns Geographische Mitteilungen, MIX, no. 4 (1965), 305.

TABLE 7. Membership in the Society of German-Soviet Friendship, 1947-65

Year	Membership
1947	2,200
1948	19,166
1949	69,707
1950	1,962,569
1953	3,119,881
1956	3,484,390
1959	3,452,607
1962	3,525,645
1965	3,432,310

Source: Statistisches Jahrbuch der DDR 1964, p. 564, *Statistisches Jahrbuch der DDR 1966,* p. 591.

119

TABLE 8. The Development of East German Foreign Trade, 1947-50

Year	Total	Import	Export	Share of the East Bloc in Total Returns
	(millions of dollars)			%
1947	102.7	—	—	26.5
1948	322.5	—	—	74.9
1949	662.0	355	307	77.1
1950	947.0	507	440	86.1

Source: Konstantin Pritzel, *Die wirtschaftliche Integration der sowjetischen Besatzungszone Deutschlands in den Ostblock und ihre politische Aspekte* (Bonn and Berlin: Bundesministerium für Gesamtdeutsche Fragen, 1962), p. 27.

TABLE 9. Types of Ownership, 1950-55

Type of Ownership	1950	1951	1952	1953	1954	1955
	(% gross production)					
State (VEB)	74.9	77.1	78.5	82.6	82.8	83.1
Joint (state and private)	1.6	1.9	2.2	2.3	2.2	2.2
Private	23.5	21.0	19.3	15.1	15.0	14.7

Source: Konstantin Pritzel, *Die wirtschaftliche Integration der sowjetischen Besatzungszone Deutschlands in den Ostblock und ihre politische Aspekte* (Bonn and Berlin: Bundesministerium für Gesamtdeutsche Fragen, 1962), p. 18.

TABLE 10. Development of Agricultural Collectivization in the G.D.R., 1952-63

Year	Number of Agrarian Collectives (LPG)	Area	Area of Total Arable Land
		(*hectares*)	(%)
1952	1,906	218,043	3.3
1953	4,461	754,301	11.6
1954	5,120	931,393	14.5
1955	6,047	1,279,200	19.7
1956	6,281	1,500,686	23.2
1957	6,691	1,631,882	25.2
1958	9,637	2,386,020	37.0
1959	10,132	2,794,306	43.5
1960	19,345	5,384,365	85.0
1961	17,860	5,430,517	84.6
1962	16,625	5,460,141	85.4
1963	16,314	5,456,143	85.6

Source: Handbuch der Deutschen Demokratischen Republik (East Berlin: Staatsverlag, n.d.), p. 403.

TABLE 11. G.D.R.—Communist Bloc Treaties (Bilateral)

Country	1949	1950	1951	1952	1953	1954	1955	1956	1957	1958	1959	1960	1961	1962	Totals
Albania	1	0	2	3	7	1	3	3	9	3	6	3	6	1	48
Bulgaria	1	5	5	2	7	4	15	2	5	13	7	4	3	1	74
Czechoslovakia	1	11	3	2	9	7	11	14	9	8	8	10	2	1	96
Hungary	2	7	4	5	4	4	9	6	13	9	3	13	2	2	83
Poland	2	11	6	8	6	11	10	8	18	10	7	5	2	4	108
Rumania	1	5	1	5	5	2	7	3	7	5	7	1	4	1	54
U.S.S.R.	3	7	4	4	12	6	13	14	17	17	4	8	4	3	116
Yugoslavia	0	0	0	0	0	1	1	5	4	2	3	6	3	1	26
China	1	1	3	1	8	6	7	3	3	3	5	5	2	0	48
Mongolia	0	1	0	0	1	0	3	1	4	3	5	3	3	1	25
N. Korea	1	0	0	2	4	1	5	4	4	2	3	3	3	1	33
N. Vietnam	0	0	0	0	0	1	0	4	4	7	4	1	3	1	25
Cuba	0	0	0	0	0	0	0	0	0	0	0	8	2	1	11
Yearly total:	13	48	28	32	63	44	84	67	97	82	62	70	39	18	747

Source: Lothar Kapsa, *Zusammenstellung der von der "Deutschen Demokratischen Republik" seit deren Gründung (7.10.1949) abgeschlossenen internationalen Verträge und Vereinbarungen,* 3rd ed. (Bonn: Archiv für Gesamtdeutsche Fragen, 1962).

TABLE 12. Correlation Matrix of Bilateral Treaties Entered into by the German Democratic Republic, 1949-62*

	Albania	Bulgaria	China	Cuba	Czechoslovakia	Hungary	Mongolia	North Korea	North Vietnam	Poland	Rumania	U.S.S.R.	Yugoslavia
Albania	—	.171	.366	(.010)†	.170	.251	.636	.695	.399	.276	.598	.421	.388
Bulgaria	.171	—	.568	(.164)	.446	.400	.472	.398	.272	.363	.592	.579	(.067)
China	.366	.568	—	.092	.530	.236	.269	.569	(.053)	.185	.307	.381	.122
Cuba	(.010)	(.164)	.092	—	.080	.422	.242	.113	(.074)	(.312)	(.387)	(.110)	.607
Czechoslovakia	.170	.446	.530	.080	—	.607	.350	.514	.263	.535	.419	.706	.467
Hungary	.251	.400	.236	.422	.607	—	.446	.398	.253	.639	.301	.698	.537
Mongolia	.636	.472	.269	.242	.350	.446	—	.578	.607	.264	.618	.376	.601
North Korea	.695	.398	.569	.113	.514	.398	.578	—	.283	.210	.568	.602	.514
North Vietnam	.399	.272	(.053)	(.074)	.263	.253	.607	.283	—	.288	.332	.534	.554
Poland	.276	.363	.185	(.312)	.535	.639	.264	.210	.288	—	.578	.655	.121
Rumania	.598	.592	.307	(.387)	.419	.301	.618	.568	.332	.578	—	.491	.028
U.S.S.R.	.421	.579	.381	(.110)	.706	.698	.376	.602	.534	.655	.491	—	.365
Yugoslavia	.388	(.067)	.122	.607	.467	.537	.601	.514	.554	.121	.028	.365	—

*This table shows the correlation of diads. That is, it answers the question, how does the diad G.D.R.-U.S.S.R. correlate with the diad G.D.R.-Czechoslovakia? The answer is .706.

†Negative correlations in parentheses ( ).

Source: Randal L. Cruikshanks, "A Technique for Measuring Stability and Change in the East German Political System" (Paper read at the 1966 Meeting of the Pacific Northwest Political Science Association, Salem, Oregon).

TABLE 13. Support and Opposition to the East German Regime, 1962-66

Posture Toward Regime:	1962	1964	1966
		%	
Loyal	37	51	71
Opponent	28	23	14
Ambivalent/"goes along"	35	26	15
	n = 70	n = 220	n = 365

Source: Hans Apel, "Bericht über das 'Staatsgefühl' der DDR-Bevölkerung," Frankfurter Hefte, XXII, no. 3 (March, 1967), 171.

SELECTED BIBLIOGRAPHY

Books:

Dahrendorf, Ralf. *Gesellschaft und Demokratie in Deutschland.* Munich: Piper & Co. Verlag, 1965.

Fischer, Ruth. *Stalin and German Communism.* Cambridge, Mass.: Harvard University Press, 1948.

Hangen, Welles. *The Muted Revolution.* New York: Alfred Knopf, 1966.

Heidenheimer, Arnold. *The Governments of Germany.* 2nd ed. New York: T. Y. Crowell, 1966.

Leissner, Gustav. *Verwaltung und öffentlicher Dienst in der sowjetischen Besatzungszone Deutschlands.* Stuttgart and Köln: W. Kohlhammer Verlag, 1961.

Leonhard, Wolfgang. *Child of the Revolution.* Translated by C. M. Woodhouse. Chicago: H. Regnery Co., 1958.

Ludz, Peter C., ed. *Studien und Materialien zur Soziologie der DDR.* Köln and Opladen: Westdeutscher Verlag, 1964.

—————. *Parteielite im Wandel.* Köln and Opladen: Westdeutscher Verlag, 1968.

Nettl, J. P. *The Eastern Zone and Soviet Policy in Germany 1945-50.* London: Oxford University Press, 1951.

Richert, Ernst. *Macht ohne Mandat.* 2nd ed. Köln and Opladen: Westdeutscher Verlag, 1963.

—————. *Das zweite Deutschland: Ein Staat der nicht sein darf.* Gütersloh: Sigbert Mohn Verlag, 1964.

Schultz, Joachim. *Der Funktionär in der Einheitspartei.* Stuttgart and Düsseldorf: Ring-Verlag, 1956.

Stern, Carola. *Porträt einer bolschewistischen Partei.* Köln: Verlag für Politik und Wirtschaft, 1957.

————. *Ulbricht: A Political Biography.* Translated by Abe Farbstein. New York: Frederick A. Praeger, 1965.

Stolper, Wolfgang F. *The Structure of the East German Economy.* Cambridge, Mass.: Harvard University Press, 1960.

Articles and Periodicals:

Apel, Hans. "Wie sie es sehen." *Der Monat* 19 (March, 1967): 15-23.

————. "Bericht über das 'Staatsgefühl' der DDR-Bevölkerung." *Frankfurter Hefte* 22 (March, 1967): 169-78.

Elliott, James R., and Scaperlanda, Anthony. "East Germany's Liberman-type Reforms in Perspective." *The Quarterly Review of Economics and Business* 6 (Autumn, 1966): 41.

Smith, Jean Edward. "The German Democratic Republic and the West." *International Journal* 22 (Spring, 1967): 231-52.

Spittmann, Ilse, ed. *SBZ-Archiv.* Köln: Verlag für Politik und Wirtschaft.

Designed by Gerard A. Valerio
Composed in Linotype Baskerville
by Wm. J. Keller Inc.
Printed offset by Wm. J. Keller Inc.
on 50 lb. Keller Publishing Text
Bound by Wm. J. Keller Inc.